NO MORE MORE DYING:

The Conquest of Aging and the Extension of Human Life

Joel Kurtzman and Phillip Gordon

PUBLISHED BY J.P. TARCHER, INC., LOS ANGELES

Distributed by Hawthorn Books, Inc., New York

056303

To R. Buckminster Fuller, who has pulled back together many shattered fragments of the human mind.—J.K.

To my parents, Harry and Adele, with fond affection.—P.G.

We would like to thank the following people for their contributions to the manuscript: Dr. Morris Claman, Clinical Assistant Professor of Urology, UCLA, for his helpful comments on the transplantation of organs; Dr. Andrew Gordon of the University of Florida at Gainesville for his help in giving shape to the manuscript; Michael Gorniowsky, M.D., and Michael J. Quigley both of Rancho Los Amigos Hospital in Downey, California, for their time and kind answers about bionics; Susan Gross, for being in the right place at the right time; Thomas Maremaa, for raising some important questions; and Dr. Bernadine Wisnieski of the Department of Bacteriology, UCLA, for lending us her expertise in genetics.

Library of Congress Catalog Card Number: 75-32856

ISBN: 0-87477-055-6

Manufactured in the United States of America

Published by J. P. Tarcher, Inc.
9110 Sunset Blvd., Los Angeles, Calif. 90069

Published simultaneously in Canada by
Prentice-Hall of Canada, Ltd.
1870 Birchmount Rd., Scarborough, Ontario

1 2 3 4 5 6 7 8 9 0

Contents

1. The Birth of Homo Longevus

Nothing is immortal. The universe itself appears to be winding down. Solar systems dissipate and lose their organized form. Blinding suns, after billions of years, burn out and collapse. Continents crumble, mountain ranges wear away, seas dry up. Chemical compounds break down. Radioactive atoms gradually decay. Subatomic particles go out of existence.

Of man's mortality, we are well aware. The first indisputably true statement of logic is "all men are mortal." Of that mortality there has been exacting documentation.

In the United States, according to Public Health Service figures, out of any 100 people starting at birth, six will die by age forty, another four by age fifty, and another nine by age sixty. By age seventy-five, half of the 100 people will be gone. After that the death rate really speeds up, so that by age eighty-five only 10 of the 100 are left; and virtually everyone is dead by age ninety. In America, the centenarian is an anomaly: there are only 13,000 in the entire country of 203 million people. Only six people in a hundred thousand live to be 100 or more.

At age twelve our bodies are so strong, say gerontologists, that if we could physically stay twelve all our lives, it would take 700 years before our bodies deteriorated to the point where they could no longer carry on the life process. However, after age thirty, as cells and cell components break down and the body diminishes in its ability to repair itself, the likelihood of our dying doubles every eight years

As we grow older, each day thousands of cells cease to function and the systems in the body begin to deteriorate. Blood vessels, tendons, and connective tissues lose their elasticity. Circulation slows down, affecting our blood pressure, mental acuity, and sense of balance. Kidneys, liver, and digestive organs degenerate, and we become increasingly susceptible to disease. Motor nerves no longer convey stimuli as fast, and our reactions become slower. Muscles lose their strength and resiliency. Joints stiffen. Bones become brittle.

These inner changes are reflected in our outward appearance. The skin becomes wrinkled and rough, with dark spots. The hair becomes white, dry, and thin. Loss of teeth shortens the lower part of the face, so that the nose droops closer to the chin. There are also changes in the skeleton; as the vertebrae come closer together, the spine is bowed and chest measurements diminish.

Vision and hearing, which begin their decline at age twelve, become greatly altered. As the lens in the eye yellows, it screens out blue, violet, and green colors, so that to the elderly paintings in blues and greens seem drab and grey. The lens also becomes stiffer and harder to focus. As hearing declines, high-frequency sounds become inaudible. Other senses also change: touch is less sensitive, and with only a sixth as many taste buds as when we were younger, we tend to prefer foods that are more seasoned.

Every day of our lives our brain cells die, never to be replaced. Between the ages of twenty and ninety, it is estimated that we lose 30 percent of the 8 to 10 billion nerve cells in our brain. In the new brain, neurons stand like young saplings, then grow to maturity (around age twenty-five) into an amazing intergrowth of hairlike branches connecting millions of nerve cells. But as the years go by, the neurons change shape: the tiny hairs swell and become lumpy, and finally at senility the branches fall off, leaving a nerve shaft that is drooping and almost bare.

As a result, we age mentally. Although some writers and artists are still going strong in their later years and although in some occupations experience is preferred to quick reflexes, mathematicians and physicists seem to do their best work under the age of thirty-five. Albert Einstein, for example, published his *Special Theory of Relativity* at age twenty-six, and was the most famous scientist in the world by age thirty. But by the time he was thirty-three he no longer produced papers of great scientific worth. Although he claimed the insights were still there, his mathematical "sense" was apparently diminished, and whenever he published papers thereafter, he would later issue retractions, acknowledging that his mathematical reasoning was incomplete. The same decline has been noted in other scientific and intellectual endeavors. Dr. Leonard Hayflick, a pioneer in genetic research, has stated that among scientists creativity peaks at about age thirty-three.

Researchers have also observed loss of psychological resilience and adaptability. When they are thirty, people begin to go through a very predictable period of lack of adaptability, the hallmark of growth and survival. Both men and women become inflexible, less willing to experiment with life. Security becomes the goal rather than innovation.

But need such decline and deterioration really be human destiny? Might it be possible to maintain our bodies at the state of cellular vigor of a twelve-year-old? Is it necessary to consider aging and death inevitable? Aging, after all, is the alteration or gradual cessation of normal processes, which brings about the increased likelihood of illness and death. It is in effect a progressive disease. Is it not possible, therefore, that as a disease it can be arrested? Can we perhaps be immunized against it? Can it be reversed?

In 1972 Dr. Alex Comfort—a famous gerontologist, but popularly known for authoring *The Joy of Sex*—told a meeting of the Gerontology Society of the United States, "I am confident techniques for slowing and reversing the aging process are close at hand." And in 1973 he said, "If the scientific and medical resources of the United States alone were mobilized, aging could be conquered within a decade."

This may seem like extraordinary optimism, but one way to

view the progress of medicine and its accompanying technologies in the last few decades is to repeat the observation of French philosopher-physician Jean Bernard. If a doctor were to fall asleep in 1900 and wake up in 1930, Bernard pointed out, he could probably have resumed practicing medicine immediately, because it would have changed so little. However, if he fell asleep in 1930 and woke up in 1960, he would have been completely out of touch. Because of the tremendous gains in medical knowledge, he would have known less about treating patients than would most first-year medical students. In 1930, for example, there were no antibiotics with which to treat syphilis, pneumonia, scarlet fever, and meningitis, to mention just a few diseases. And in the less than two decades since 1960 the advance of medical procedures and technology has accelerated. Particularly there has been tremendous progress in treating many age-related maladies, such as high blood pressure, glaucoma, arthritis, cataracts, and heart damage. Where only a few years ago no healing techniques existed, procedures with a high degree of success today are commonplace.

If a physician fell asleep today, to awaken at the end of this century—not much over two decades away—he would just as surely awaken to procedures which may now be thought of as impossible. A recent report makes some dramatic predictions. From time to time, the Economics Department of McGraw-Hill Publications in New York surveys scientific researchers, planners, and forecasters in twelve major industries and asks them to consider a series of technological developments, to estimate the date of a breakthrough, its economic feasibility, and widespread use. In the "Third Survey of Technological Breakthroughs and Widespread Application of Significant Technical Developments," released in October 1975, scientists predicted the following occurrences by the year 2000—and some well before then:

—There will be drugs to cure or prevent cancer.
—A practical substitute for blood will be available.
—There will be artificial eyesight for the blind.
—Senility will be controlled by chemicals and drugs.
—Drugs will be available to permanently raise the level of intelligence.

    —Cryogenics—human hibernation and refrigeration—will be a reality.

    —Chemical control over some hereditary characteristics will have been accomplished through molecular engineering.

    —The aging process will have been chemically controlled.

    —There will be engineering of human genetic processes.

These are not isolated, wild-eyed speculations. In 1964, in a survey taken by the Rand Corporation in Santa Monica, California, eighty-two of the world's foremost gerontologists said that by 1992 science would be able to add at least twenty years to the human life span. This means that living 20 to 40 percent longer than we do now may soon be within our grasp.

Moreover the Rand-polled scientists perceived a "synergetic effect," whereby one antiaging or life-extending breakthrough would give a person enough extra time to live until a subsequent discovery might extend his life span even more. Indeed, as we shall see by the end of this book, many such situations already exist.

We are without doubt—for good or bad—standing at the gate of a new era, when *Homo sapiens* will be medically transformed into *Homo longevus*—extremely long-lived men and women who still retain their mental and physical vigor. If this is so, it demands an entirely new perception of life.

2. In Search of Five-Score Years and Ten

How long can a person live? What accounts for the differences in longevity between people? Are there "secrets" to attaining long life, and can these secrets be applied to ourselves? Answers to all of these questions emerge from many different disciplines.

The orderly study of the human life span goes back to the late seventeenth century, when it was initiated by the English astronomer Edmund Halley, discoveror of Halley's Comet. In an attempt to find mathematical regularities that would yield insight into the possible length of life, Halley took the death records for the Polish city of Breslau (then a part of Germany), and constructed a table (called a life-table) showing how many people died at each particular age. For the average Breslau citizen, he determined, life expectancy was about thirty-four years.

During the eighteenth and nineteenth centuries, the study of human life span was most advanced by mathematicians working for life insurance companies, who were interested in making an exact determination of life expectancy so that they would know how much to charge in premiums to guarantee a profit on most of their policies. The first mathematician to formulate life-tables for insurance purposes was James Dodson, who in 1756 invited businessmen to meet with him at the Queen's Head Tavern in London to discuss a scientifically based set of premiums calculated through the use of life-tables. Out of these meetings grew the first life insurance company to operate on the principles of mathematical study of human life span, the Equitable Life Assurance Society, organized in 1762.

Early actuarial work was inexact, for such life-tables were developed from unreliable and incomplete information, as the recording of births and deaths was not compulsory in most countries. It was not until 1837 that England, for example, required that all births, deaths, and marriages be recorded through the General Register Office. Even so, the development of life-tables went on, and early nineteenth century mathematicians began to notice a regular pattern—namely, that the probability that a person would die increased, in *regular* fashion, with the age of that person. This observation, which seems so obvious today, led them to speculate that there might be a biological "law of mortality" acting in nature, which could be expressed by some mathematical connection between age and the probability of dying. The first person to specify this "law of mortality" was English mathematician Benjamin Gompertz who, in 1825, devised a formula to express the increasing probability of death with age. From this formula, Gompertz was able to draw a graph that showed the theoretical maximum age that humans could attain. That maximum, he determined, was 100 to 110 years.

Compared to the ages of other animals in nature, even 100 years is a very big figure. Few other living things survive longer than man. Reflecting on the death of the well-known painter of primitives, Grandma Moses, at age 101, scientist-writer Isaac Asimov asked, "How many living things that greeted the day and responded to the changing environment at the moment of [her] birth in 1860 were still doing so on the day of her death in 1961? The list is tiny."

The oldest living things are trees such as redwoods. Perhaps one of the oldest trees is a bald cypress in Tula, Mexico, believed to be almost 7,000 years old. Some giant tortoises live to be 200 years or so. No other creatures top the century mark. And trees and tortoises, Asimov points out, buy longevity at the price of passivity or of very cold-blooded slow motion. Man, by contrast, is warm-blooded, and "is as fast-moving and deft as any creature alive. He races through life and yet manages to outlive all organisms that, like him, race, and almost all organisms that, unlike him, crawl or are motionless."

The life spans of some animals mentioned by Asimov, in *The Human Body,* are as follows: Shrew—1½ years. Rat—4 to 5 years. Rabbit—up to 15 years. Dog—up to 18. Pig—up to 20. Horse—up to 40. Chimpanzee—to late 30s. Gorilla—to late 40s. Elephant—up to 70. In general, the larger the mammal, the longer-lived. But there are exceptions—the most astonishing being man, who is smaller than a horse and smaller than an elephant, yet can outlive both.

Setting aside the maximum human life span figures for the moment, let us look at those that relate more to each of us—namely, those for an *average* life span. Over the past three centuries, the average life expectancy has been increasing, with particular growth occurring in this century. Halley's first life-table of the Breslau population showed that average life expectancy at birth was about thirty-four years (the same as in some African countries today, where advances in medicine and sanitation have been lacking—see the table, next page). This average did not change greatly until the nineteenth century, when it slowly began to rise until in 1900 in the United States it reached forty-seven. After that, average life expectancy increased dramatically: in 1930 it was fifty-nine; today in America it is seventy-one.

The extraordinary increase in average life expectancy in the U.S. in the twentieth century—almost 45 percent—is due mainly to advances in sanitation, public health, and medicine. At all age levels, prevention and cure have played their part. For instance, the adoption of sterilization techniques by doctors drastically reduced the deaths of women in childbirth. Treatment for such childhood killers as measles, polio, chicken pox, whooping cough, and bacterial infections also sharply reduced deaths of infants and children. In the mid-nineteenth century a baby had only a 75 percent chance of surviving to age fourteen; today the figure is 97 percent. Tuberculosis, the major cause of death for young and middle-aged adults until after the turn of the century, has been virtually eradicated. And death from the diseases of old age is constantly being forestalled.

But this dramatic increase in *average* life expectancy does not mean that people have longer maximum life spans than they did in the seventeenth century. As R. D. Clark, a respected English insurance actuary, says, death rates for older people (over eighty) "have remained stationary for as long as we have reliable records." Because of the advances in health and medicine, he says, there are "more

10 Countries with Highest Life Expectancies—and the U.S.A.

	Men	Women	Average
1. Sweden	71.8	76.5	74.2
2. The Netherlands	71.0	76.4	73.7
3. Iceland	70.8	76.2	73.5
4. Norway	71.0	76.0	73.5
5. Denmark	70.6	75.4	73.0
6. Ryukyu Islands	68.9	75.6	72.3
7. Canada	68.7	75.2	72.0
8. France	68.0	75.5	71.7
9. Japan	69.0	74.3	71.7
10. United Kingdom	68.5	74.7	71.6
U.S.A.	67.4	75.2	71.2

10 Countries with Lowest Life Expectancies

	Men	Women	Average
1. Guinea	26.0	28.0	27.0
2. Upper Volta	32.1	31.1	31.6
3. Chad	29.0	35.0	32.0
4. Angola			33.5
5. Guinea-Bissau			33.5
6. Central African Republic	33.0	36.0	34.5
7. Gabon	25.0	45.0	35.0
8. Togo	31.6	38.5	35.0
9. Burundi	35.0	38.5	36.7
10. Nigeria	37.2	36.7	36.9

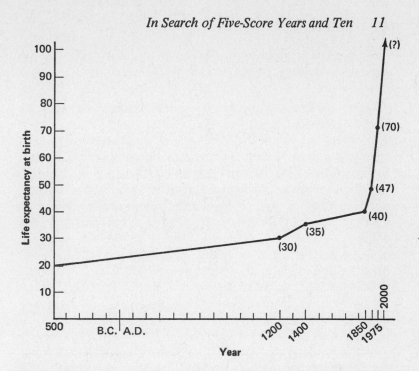

Life line. Rise in life expectancy at birth throughout recorded history.

people surviving into old age . . . but there is as yet no sign of any extension of the limit of human life."

Of course, there have been reports of individuals who have lived to be considerably older than Gompertz's 110. As medical columnist Lawrence Galton reports, in *How Long Will I Live?*, a Shropshire farmer named Thomas Parr was reputed to be 152 when he died in 1635; Joseph Burrington was supposed to be 154 when he died in Bergen, Norway, in 1790; and a woman in Knoxville, Tennessee, was said to be an amazing 160 years old when she died in 1935. But, Galton points out, "there has been some skepticism about these cases for lack of adequate documentation." Still, in the case of Louise K. Thiers, who died in 1926 in Milwaukee, Galton says, "there was satisfactory evidence that she had reached the ripe age of 111 years and 138 days."

"THE REPORTS OF MY LIFE ARE
GREATLY EXAGGERATED"

But what about those 120-year-old Russians and others we hear about? Indeed, aren't some of them even older?

There are groups of people living in three places who indeed seem to live exceptionally long: (1) the inhabitants of the Caucasus, the area between the Black and Caspian seas in the Soviet Union; (2) the Vilcabambans of southern Equador; and (3) the Hunzukuts of northeast Pakistan. Anthropologists and gerontologists report finding people among these cultures claiming to be well over 120 years old.

One man in the Caucasus, Shirali Muslimov, was said to be 168 when he died in 1973. He was survived by five living generations—including a four-year-old great-great-great grandchild and a 120-year-old widow he had married 102 years earlier. Born in 1805, according to his internal passport, he retained memories of the 1853-56 Crimean War, and until his death he tended an orchard he said he had planted in 1870. According to Soviet gerontologists, another spectacular oldster, named Tsurba, lived to celebrate her 100th wedding anniversary, and was reportedly 160 years old when she died.

However, many scientists are skeptical. Zhores A. Medvedev, a Russian geneticist now at the National Institute for Medical Research in London, feels that these reports of advanced age are based on individual exaggeration. There is no case, he says, of a person living longer than 113 years—a Frenchman named Pierre Toubert, who was born July 15, 1701, and who died November 16, 1814—that has ever been confirmed by independent documentation, such as birth or baptismal certificates. He feels that the reports of exceptional age in the Caucasus arose because long-lived people there are accorded great respect (the familiar toast is "May you live to be 300!") and because many of the old men long ago adopted their fathers' identifications in order to escape military service in the war after the 1917 Revolution and during the two world wars. Furthermore, he points out, Joseph Stalin was from the Republic of Georgia in the Caucasus, and to please him, many Soviet researchers may have accepted the reports of longevity there without corroboration. Thus, Medvedev concludes, "in most cases the phenomenon of exceptional longevity restricted by specific geographical area does not exist." Rather, he says, the phenomenon developed for many social, cultural, and political reasons and "was backed by science under conditions which normally lead to the transformation of science into pseudoscience, conditions which . . . intentionally produce only confirming information."

This research is still defended by the Russians. G. E. Pitzheglauri, director of the Gerontology Center in the capital of Georgia, says he has studied over 15,000 people of the Caucasus, all over eighty years, and has tested more than 700 centenarians, many with birth certificates or baptismal records counterchecked with careful questions of historical events, marriage and birth dates, and so on.

But regardless of exactly how long the people in the Caucasus live, it seems to be that *more people* there do live longer. In one area called Deghestan (population of about a million), 70 out of every 100,000 people were found to be 100 years old or more. This compares with only 6 in 100,000 Americans who live to that age. And in all of the Caucasus, whose population is the size of New York City's, 9½ million, there are reportedly 5,000 centenarians, compared to the only 13,000 in the entire United States with its vastly larger population (now about 210 million).

The same high proportion appears to be true of Vilcabamba, a valley of about a thousand people, 300 miles south of Quito in Equador. Their 1940 census revealed that 18 percent of the inhabitants were over sixty-five (compared to 9 percent in the U.S.) and that nine people had lived to be, supposedly, anywhere from 100 to 130 years old.

The same situation appears to exist in Hunza, a 200-mile-long valley located in the Karakoran Range in the Himalayas of northeastern Pakistan. In a population of 40,000, there are six men over 100 years of age; many are 90 or older. The highest estimate of longevity has been 150 years, but as Betty Lee Morales, who visited Hunza as president of the American Cancer Society, pointed out, that is probably an exaggeration. Still, she added, "there's no need to gild the lily. The average age is ninety when they die."

If, to paraphrase Mark Twain on learning of an obituary being mistakenly written about him, the reports of their deaths are greatly exaggerated—that is, their age at death—the fact remains that the inhabitants of the Caucasus, Vilcabamba, and Hunza live very long and, more importantly, have a *vigorous* old age. And, as we shall see, there are circumstances about the way they live that may help us to attain a physically active life and extend it beyond today's expectations.

LIVING TO FIVE-SCORE YEARS AND TEN

We are forever reading newspaper interviews with people who are celebrating their hundredth birthday. To what, the reporter always asks, does the individual attribute his longevity? God and clean living, one may reply. Smoking and drinking and having a good time, responds another. Now every centenarian is, of course, entitled to his own opinion as to how *he* (or she) got there, but it may have very little to suggest how *you* might get there.

Two factors clearly affect the length of our lives—heredity and environment. One need not be born into a long-lived family in order to be long-lived, but it helps. People with long-lived ancestors tend to have lower mortality rates at every age and a greater chance of reaching or passing eighty.

However, the influence of heredity on life span is not total. As Alex Comfort states, "longevity in man is 'hereditary' in the sense that it tends to run in families . . . there is a correlation between the ages reached by parents and the expectation of life of their children." Still, the correlation is not as complete as for, say, height; the children of long-lived people, Comfort says, are less likely to be long-lived than the children of tall people are likely to be tall.

There are perhaps 2,000 diseases and defects that are influenced by heredity—among them some types of blindness and deafness, mental retardation, hemophilia, and metabolic disorders—but such disorders are not a statistically significant cause of death. As Galton says, "while heredity is responsible for some serious diseases, they are the rare kinds. Heredity usually acts as a factor that may predispose the body toward disease, but does not make the disease inevitable."

Although we cannot choose our parents and all that we get from them, we can still control to some degree the second factor—our environment. We can try to alter our environment so as to give our inherited constitution a better chance.

In 1973 the National Center for Health Statistics of the Public Health Service in Washington, D.C., published a table (see below) that reflects how long we could live if some of the major killers were eliminated. If we could put an end to the diseases of the arteries and the heart, we would gain, on the average, an extra 17.5 years. If we were to cut out 80 percent of the cancer in this country, we would extend our lives by another 2.5 years. If we were to dramatically reduce the number of deaths by murder, accident, suicide, cirrhosis of the liver, influenza, and diabetes, we could add another 2.5 years to our lives. If we were to eliminate all these life shorteners, many of

Gain in Years in Expectation of Life
If Cause Was Eliminated (at Birth)

Cause of Death	Gain in Years
Major cardiovascular-renal diseases	10.9
Heart diseases	5.9
Vascular diseases affecting the central nervous system	1.3
Malignant neoplasms	2.3
Accidents, excluding those caused by motor vehicles	0.6
Motor vehicle accidents	0.6
Influenza and pneumonia	0.5
Infectious diseases (excluding tuberculosis)	0.2
Diabetes mellitus	0.2
Tuberculosis	0.1

SOURCE: Life tables published by the National Center of Health Statistics, U.S. Public Health Service and U.S. Bureau of the Census, "Some Demographic Aspects of Aging in the United States," February 1973.

them self-generated by our living styles or environmentally caused, we would add, on the average, 22.5 years to all of our lives. The average man would live to be 92.5 and the average woman to 97.5. And much of this is possible without the invention of any new medications, treatments, or technical advances in medicine. Indeed, most of it is within our own immediate control, and is a function of our daily habits, as a survey of these elements will quickly show.

Smoking

Cigarette smoking is responsible for over 95 percent of all lung, throat, and tongue cancer, plus a great percentage of cases of emphysema. Men who smoke are twice as likely to experience heart attacks as nonsmokers. If you smoke two or more packs a day, you are essentially trading a minute of life for a minute of smoking; you can expect to lose 8.3 years of life compared to a nonsmoker. Insurance companies know this, or they wouldn't offer reductions in premiums for nonsmokers.

Drinking

Although alcohol in moderation is probably not a life short-ener (indeed Dr. Lester Breslow, Dean of the School of Public Health at UCLA, found that moderate drinkers live longer than either heavy drinkers or nondrinkers), more than one or two drinks a day expose a person to three of the ten highest causes of death: cirrhosis of the liver, motor vehicle death, and pneumonia. Drinking in excess may also lead to heart disease through weakening of the heart muscle, as well as to ulcers, high blood pressure, diabetes, asthma, gout, neuritis, and anemia. Alcohol is not only involved in about half of all serious traffic accidents, it is also a factor in many murders, especially where murderer and victim know each other.

Drugs and Chemicals

There are 50,000 drugs, 36,000 pesticides, and 7,000 food additives, not to mention thousands of other chemicals used in the

United States today. Many of them enter our bodies in our food and from the air. By changing your habits, you can take some steps to diminish the reported dangers. Heavy coffee consumption, for example, may lead to ulcers; birth control pills, in women over forty, appears to make them five times more likely to have a fatal heart attack than women not taking the pill. Other chemicals, like those in processed foods or in your immediate environment, may be more difficult to avoid. Drinking soft water is more apt to lead to heart disease than is drinking hard water. Death rates in areas with dense air pollution are much higher than those in pollution-free neighborhoods. Indeed, according to one medical review, if air pollution levels were cut in half, bronchitis cases would be reduced 25 to 50 percent, heart disease by 20 percent, and cancer 15 percent.

Weight

Figures from the National Center for Health Statistics show that you lose about a year of life for every ten pounds of excess fat you carry. In addition, overweight people—an estimated 25 percent of all Americans—are three and a half times likelier to have fatal heart attacks and strokes as are people of normal weight. They are also subject to kidney disease, diabetes, cirrhosis of the liver, cancer of the liver and gallbladder, respiratory infection, high blood pressure, and a host of other disorders.

Diet

Coronary heart disease has been shown to be seven times greater in people with high cholesterol levels and high triglyceride blood levels. By cutting down on beef, eggs, butter, ice cream, and hard cheese, and by increasing the intake of fish, veal, poultry, vegetables, fruits, cereals, and low-saturated fat margarines, one has only one-third the chance of a heart attack as a person on a standard American diet. Dr. Hans Kugler of Roosevelt University of Chicago says that he believes bad nutrition decreases the average life span approximately six to ten years.

Exercise

Kugler also estimates that a good exercise program (which he defines as two 2-hour sessions per week that include such vigorous exercises as jogging, rowing, tennis, swimming) slows physical deterioration and can add six to nine years to average life expectancy. In addition, exercise eases tension, lowers cholesterol levels and blood pressure, and toughens the heart muscle. As Dr. Alexander Leaf of Harvard Medical School says, "exercise is the closest thing to an antiaging pill." Statistics of the Metropolitan Life Insurance Company of New York show that at most ages major league baseball players, for example, are 30 percent less likely to die than other people the same age. Although there are those such as Dr. Lawrence Morehouse of UCLA who feel that even thirty minutes a week of exercise is enough to tone the body and elevate the heartbeat rate, others believe that exercise must be carried out consistently—an hour a day, six days a week—to be beneficial.

Regular Medical Examinations

Detecting a disease before it becomes serious is a proven life extender. Men over forty who have an annual physical checkup can expect to add two years to their lives, according to most insurance companies. Women over thirty who have an annual exam (including breast exam and Pap smear) can add four years to their lives.

Change, Stress, and Distress

For most people, change, stress, and tension are life-shorteners. The pioneering work of Dr. Thomas Holmes of the University of Washington School of Medicine has shown that almost any significant change in your life may increase your chances of getting sick—and not only change for the worse (death of a spouse, minor violation of the law, trouble with one's boss), but also change for the better (vacation, marriage, promotion). Severe emotional stress as a result of too many quickly accumulated life changes, Holmes concluded, was invariably the precursor to disease. Hans

Selye of the University of Montreal was one of the first physicians to recognize the role of stress on longevity. He writes, "it is immaterial whether the agent or situation we face is pleasant or unpleasant; all that counts is the intensity of the demand [on the body] for readjustment."

These findings have been reconfirmed by many researchers. Richard Rahe, a research psychiatrist at the Navy Medical Neuropsychiatric Research Unit in San Diego, found that highly stressed people undergoing a life crisis may have a higher probability of dying earlier. "It appears that death," he says, "rather than coming on unpredictably in life, may well follow a major life crisis." In addition, behavioral stress profiles seem to show that competitive and impatient people—the kind who finish other people's sentences or curse at slow drivers in front of them—are particularly prone to heart attacks.

There are countless other life choice and environmental factors that influence life span:

—Dr. Robert Samp of the University of Wisconsin surveyed 2,000 long-lived people and found that good health was related to personality traits such as moderation, serenity, optimism, interest in others as well as in the future.

—A study in West Germany indicated that one year of unemployment may reduce the life expectancy of a job loser by five years, and it is well known that for many people retirement literally kills.

—Research by Dr. Erdman B. Palmore of Duke University Medical Center indicates that job satisfaction is even more important than physical functioning and not smoking in determining longevity.

—Living arrangements also contribute to one's physical wellbeing. People who live with a spouse or a friend survive longer than those who live alone.

For the long-lived inhabitants of the Caucasus, Vilcabamba, and Hunza, many of the healthful disciplines and life styles come with their culture. In the Caucasian diet, for instance, sugar is rarely used, salt intake is low, and cholesterol-producing animal fats are eaten infrequently. The diet consists principally of fresh produce, meats, and milk; overeating is virtually unknown. The meals in Vilcabamba are similarly simple; indeed, the average person's calorie intake is only half that of most Americans. The Hunza diet is likewise minimal in animal fat, cholesterol, and calories.

In all three cultures, life is hard, but it keeps people physically active. A Hunzukut farmer sometimes climbs a thousand-foot path several times a day to perform his tasks. Aged Vilcabambans continue to shepherd flocks of sheep, weed fields, chafe grain.

Equally important, life is relatively unchanging in these cultures. According to Sula Benet, professor emeritus of anthropology at Hunter College in New York and author of *How To Live To Be 100: The Life-Style of the People of the Caucasus,* their cultural behavior emphasizes moderation, consistency, and continuity in behavior and relationships. Thus, conflict and stress are minimized. The Vilcabambans also live extremely quiet lives, with few worries, and Hunza has a similarly relaxed atmosphere.

With it all we come back to the fact that probably no one knows for certain what the maximum life span of man currently is. Some geneticists such as Leonard Hayflick, formerly of Stanford University, who have based their hypothesis on the rate of cell deterioration, believe it is between 110 and 120 years. It seems, then, as though Gompertz's figure of about 110 is essentially correct—today. Tomorrow, however, this may be the age of youth.

Dr. Justus Shifferes of the Health Education Council of New York maintains that "If human beings, attaining full physical stature at twenty-five, were to follow the same curve of slow decay as many of the lower animals, mankind should enjoy an average *normal* life span of 150 years." This is, of course, more than *double* the average life span we have now. Roosevelt's Hans Kugler is even more optimistic. "If you could prevent only 10 percent of the aging factors," he says, "and undo another 10 percent of the damage already done, your maximum life expectancy would be approximately 280 to 340 years."

The rest of this book is concerned with exploring how, through science and medicine, this longevity in full vigor might well come about. In the next chapter, however, we need to take a detour to look at some unconventional remedies that have been suggested for rejuvenation and retarding disease and aging.

3. The Youth Doctors

The search for a way to restore youth and vigor and extend life goes back long before Isabella and Ferdinand dispatched Ponce de Leon to find the Fountain of Youth. In an attempt to lengthen life and increase strength, the Egyptians and Romans ate garlic in massive quantities. The emperors of China during the time of Confucius hired alchemists, who prescribed precise doses of gold and mercury—considered everlasting because they appeared not to tarnish, although mercury is in fact highly poisonous—to extend their lives. Alchemy spread to Europe, and during the Middle Ages such men as Francis Bacon, the British philosopher and author, and Paracelsus, the Swiss-born "father of modern medicine," practiced it, seeking the magical Philosopher's Stone that would transmute lead into gold and mortals into immortals. Many Europeans also tried plant remedies such as the root of the mandrake plant, a relative of the potato which grows in the unusual shape of a tiny man with outstretched limbs and which was supposed to issue a shriek when harvested. A narcotic (and also a poison), the mandrake root was thought to restore sexual potency. Insects were also popular antiaging remedies; Spanish Fly, made from the Blister Beetle, was not only considered an aphrodisiac but also a sexual rejuvenator, although in fact it did nothing but produce tremendous irritation and itching in urethras and bladders.

The obvious connection between sexual vitality and rejuvenation processes brought about some strange rejuvenation medicine in the early 1920s.

THE MONKEY CONNECTION

Serge Voronoff was a Russian doctor who was for a time the personal physician to the Khedive Abbas II of Egypt. In that capacity he noticed that the castrated Eunuchs guarding the Khedive's harem were in need of almost constant medical attention. As a result of this observation, he wrote later, it became apparent to him that "the physical and intellectual qualities of animals and of men are as intimately conditioned by the hormones secreted by the testicles as are the secondary sex characteristics [such as beard growth]."

Voronoff viewed sex hormone production as the key to youth and vitality, and after he left the Khedive's service he began an active search for men whose testicular endowment and need for money were sufficiently large to compel them to sell their organs for transplant research. Extensive advertising in France, where he had moved in 1919, brought him only two volunteers, and they stated such a high price for their sacrifice that Voronoff decided to obtain the glands from monkeys instead.

By the 1920s, after he had found suitable simian specimens in the Belgian and British African colonies, he began to attract clients. Between the years 1920 and 1927, over a thousand elderly men received transplants of monkey sexual organs as a form of rejuvenation therapy—each at a fee of $5,000. When he died in 1951, it was estimated that Voronoff's total income throughout his career amounted to $10 million.

Voronoff was not the only sex gland practitioner. In the United States, John Romulus Brinkly specialized in transplanting goat testicles into elderly males (for a more modest fee of $750).

Like Voronoff, Brinkly did very well at it, and was able to buy a radio station and make enormous campaign contributions to his state's politicians. He was almost elected governor of Kansas, before his practice was closed down by the state's Board of Medical Registration and Examination in 1942.

Their cures were, of course, fraudulent, but Voronoff particularly left an enduring legacy. The prized monkeys he had cultivated for transplant purposes had years earlier developed syphilis and had transmitted the disease not only to every newly arrived animal in the cage but also to the old gentlemen who had received the transplanted organ. Paul Niehans, a Swiss endocrinologist who was also interested in rejuvenation, told Voronoff he should have used testes from bulls instead. Bulls do not get syphilis.

THE CELEBRITY WAY TO REJUVENATION

Paul Niehans, who became the most famous of the modern youth doctors, claimed his mother was an illegitimate daughter of King Frederick III of Prussia. In his Swiss Alps house (called Sonnenfels—"rock in the sun"—a house once owned by Haile Selassie) he displayed pictures of the king, along with medieval religious portraits, Dürer engravings, and testimonials from some of his 50,000 patients. Among these patients were some of the best known people in the world: Pope Pius XII, Winston Churchill, Charles de Gaulle, Konrad Adenauer, W. Somerset Maugham, Gloria Swanson, Thomas Mann, and Bernard Baruch.

Niehans, who held an M.D. as well as a Ph.D in theology, specialized in rejuvenation through a process he called "cell therapy," which he defined as "a selective form of treatment which aims at developing underdeveloped organs or organs which are not capable of regenerating themselves."

He claimed to have discovered the treatment accidentally one day in 1931 when he was called to a hospital to treat a woman whose parathyroid glands had been excised by mistake during an operation for removal of a goiter. Goiter occurs when the thyroid gland, located in the neck, has become enlarged by disease. The parathyroid glands are four tiny lumps of tissue imbedded in the thyroid gland, and without them, a person quickly loses control of his muscles, begins to have convulsions, becomes rigid, and soon dies. Although this is a treatable situation now, in 1931 there were no hormones available that could be injected into the woman to take the place of those produced by the removed parathyroid glands.

As Niehans drove to the hospital, he said later, he realized there was nothing he could do to save the woman's life. Then, quite suddenly he remembered an old principle expressed by Paracelsus in the sixteenth century—*treat like with like*. At that instant, Niehans changed direction and headed for a nearby slaughterhouse, where he had been performing experiments on laboratory animals. A steer was slaughtered, its parathyroid glands removed and packed in ice, and Niehans continued to the hospital, where he then quickly minced the animal's parathyroids into pieces, mixed them in a sterile solution, and injected the substance into the woman's chest. The results were spectacular. The patient's convulsions and cramps immediately slackened and in two hours disappeared altogether. And they did not recur.

How did this happen? No one was more surprised than Niehans himself. As he told Patrick McGrady, author of *The Youth Doctors,* "I had thought that the action would be no more than that of a hormone injection, with a brief relief and a need for repeated treatments. But, surprise! Not only did it fail to provide any unpleasant reaction in the patient, but it acted in a lasting way."

There was nothing truly revolutionary in Niehans' treatment. As an endocrinologist, he knew that the injection of pure steer hormones into a person had become a relatively safe and common procedure, and since the 1920s, physicians had been obtaining insulin (the hormone that controls sugar utilization in the body) for injection into diabetics. But Niehans based his explanation of his cure on the "sympathetic magic" of like healing like, and claimed that the steer cells caused the regeneration of excised glandular tissue.

Later, as he experimented with injecting the cells from unborn lambs into the bodies of people suffering from the degeneration that comes with age, he became more and more convinced that cell therapy was a true rejuvenator. News of his treatment drew thousands of people to his Clinique La Prarie, near Vevey in Switzerland, and Niehans himself became as celebrated as his famous clients.

The search for eternal youth at La Prarie was expensive (in 1937 the price was $1,500 for each series of injections of lamb placenta cells—all tests extra) and the routine was well worked out. A patient would arrive on a weekend, and on Monday would be given an Alberhalden Resistance Reaction Ferment Test—a urine test that Niehans said measured the individual output and functional capacity of each organ in the body. On Thursday, after the Alberhalden test was analyzed, pregnant sheep would be slaughtered, the lamb embryos taken out and their organs removed, and the patient would be injected with cells taken from the appropriate animal organ—heart for heart, liver for liver—in accordance with the theory of treating like with like.

Later, refinements in the technique were added. Niehans began freeze-drying the organs, using the same procedures by which coffee is freeze-dried—indeed, Niehans got the idea from Nestle, the Swiss coffee and chocolate manufacturer. This allowed him to pulverize and quick-freeze organs removed from the sheep embryos and thereby preserve their freshness and avoid wasting organs not needed by particular patients.

Did Niehans' treatments work? He maintained the strictest secrecy over who his patients were, but the most famous of them became known. Thomas Mann lived to be eighty. Pope Pius XII lived to be eighty-two. Somerset Maugham lived to be ninety-one, and Bernard Baruch lived to be ninety-five. And when Niehans himself died, in 1971, he was eighty-nine.

Clinique La Prarie still operates and is now headed by Niehans's former assistant, Dr. Walter Michel. Cell therapy is illegal in the U.S., where it is considered dangerous by the American Medical Association (treatments may cause infection or may elicit an immune response from the body), but it is practiced in various clinics in Mexico, Argentina, France, Belgium, Italy, Holland, West Germany, and England.

Currently the leading practitioner in Great Britain is Peter Stephan, who calls his treatment "body servicing." His London clinic attracts clients from all over the world willing to pay around

$600 for the "revitalization body servicing" or for relief of "stress and strain," and lesser amounts for "geriatrics (treatment of aging and rheumatism)," "impotence and sexual conditions (male)," and the menopause in females. Stephan says he bases his treatments on the fact that "experiments throughout the world have shown the importance of one substance, ribonucleic acid (RNA), as the factor essential for new tissue growth and regeneration." Body servicing, according to Stephan's literature, "uses specific preparations containing the individual RNA of organs." It also includes "serotherapy," a method of treatment that uses "specific serums obtained through antigen-antibody reactions."

Before therapy is undertaken, Stephan, like Niehans, sends a patient's urine sample to Germany for an Alberhalden test, and analyzes his blood samples. Following that, treatment is given, either by a course of injections or by suppositories. In the case of geriatrics, for instance, the treatment consists of a preparation containing "the RNA from placenta, testicle, ovary, suprarenal cortex, hypothalamus, pituitary thalamus, liver, spleen, kidney, heart, blood vessels, and cerebral cortex." These freeze-dried cells are manufactured by a company in Heidelberg, Germany, under the guidelines set down by Niehans.

Stephan is not a medical doctor, but under British law the practice of medicine is not confined simply to physicians. While a self-styled "physician" may not work for National Health, as long as he does not prescribe drugs considered dangerous, practice certain procedures (such as full anesthesia or heart surgery), or do other things specifically restricted to M.D.s, it is permissible to practice medicine. Even surgical operations on the skin and eyes are legitimate if only local anesthetics are used. Cell therapy falls in this category.

What are the results of body servicing? Stephan says that "Patients report they feel generally better and more alert, they look and feel younger and have better physical and mental capabilities." The servicing of the body to prevent disease and premature aging makes both men and women, he says, look younger and have fewer age lines and better figures.

It is not possible to do a close analysis of the results of cell therapy and body servicing. Neither Niehans nor Stephan have published papers giving the details of their successes and failures.

Their patients may seem to be long-lived, but we know only of the patients they have chosen to make public—they have not released records of those who died at fifty or younger. Even though many of the patients have lived longer than average lives, there are reasons apart from cell therapy why this could be so. First, they may have taken good care of themselves, as evidenced by the fact that they had enough concern about their health and longevity to seek treatment. Second, they sought treatment later in life while still in good health—Niehans, at least, didn't treat *sick* people, only those complaining of "body fatigue," "impotence," etc. Third, the relatively healthy fifty-five-year-olds and over who came to Niehans already stood a good chance of living long since they had already lived through the more dangerous years when one is more likely to die from accident, heart attack, and so on. Fourth, the clients in the main were also fairly well off, and their ability to obtain and benefit from the best of orthodox medical care also enhanced their life spans. Finally, they may have been helped along not because of the cell therapy but because of their *belief* in the cell therapy—the placebo effect.

Niehans and Stephan's work has been much criticized. For example, science writer Paul Ferris in the *New York Times* says that the famous Alberhalden test, their essential diagnostic tool, "is scientifically meaningless." But critics do not diminish the appeal of youthfulness. Dr. Robert Charthams, a sexology writer for *Penthouse* magazine, underwent the Stephan clinic treatment. When confronted by Ferris about its lack of scientific validity, he responded, "Frankly, I don't care a bugger how it works. Is it possible to regenerate cells? Medically speaking, I would think not. But there must be something in it."

It is doubtful that there is. Although Stephan has stated that no one has ever died from the treatment, the question remains as to whether anyone has lived longer because of it.

THE ROMANIAN YOUTH DRUG

In Romania it is possible to get one's "youth shots" from government doctors. These shots do not contain animal cells or RNA; they contain the common anesthetic procaine.

The substance, called Gerovital (made up of procaine hydrochloride and haematoporphyrin), was developed in 1945 by Dr. Ana Aslan, M.D. of the Bucharest Institute of Geriatrics. Aslan had originally been using the drug to help elderly patients with arthritis, but she noticed that Gerovital also improved their memories, muscular strength, and skin texture, and actually caused their gray hair to regain some color. In conjunction with the government, she established 144 treatment centers throughout Romania, offering Gerovital injections in recreational surroundings, and charging $430 for a two-week stay. Over the last twenty-five years Aslan has claimed to have cured people of wrinkles, gray hair, deafness, arthritis, heart disease, and impotence.

This kind of treatment—available to American movie stars and notables like Charles de Gaulle, as well as to the Romanians themselves—has so much resembled the Niehans treatment and that of other celebrity youth doctors that it has made gerontologists skeptical about the validity of the claims for the rejuvenating effects of Gerovital. But some American researchers, such as Dr. Tom Yau of the Ohio Mental Health and Mental Retardation Research Center in Cleveland, began accumulating evidence that Gerovital might be useful, especially in the treatment of depression, and as a result in 1972 the Food and Drug Administration authorized testing on the drug as an antidepressant. Some studies also seemed to show that Gerovital could sometimes improve such age-damaged mental conditions as loss of short-term memory in elderly psychiatric patients.

The upshot of these investigations was that Gerovital seemed so promising that American researchers invited Aslan to speak at a 1974 conference on theoretical aspects of aging, sponsored by the University of Miami's Graduate Training Program in Cellular Aging. At this conference, Aslan recommended that preventative treatment with Gerovital be started at age forty-five, and said it had tremendously beneficial effects in helping older people regain and maintain physical and mental health.

But she admitted that so far she had been unable to demonstrate that Gerovital could prolong the lives of older people, saying only that "as work with Gerovital continues in the United States, more issues as to its . . . importance will be clarified." One conference participant was more cautious in making judgments, as apparently were many others. "Very few scientists are prepared to say the drug can keep you young, even a little," said Dr. Ruth Weg of the Andrus Gerontology Center of the University of Southern California. "We just don't know."

REGENERESEN THERAPY

Another current youth treatment, Regeneresen therapy or RNA therapy was developed by Dr. Benjamin S. Frank, a Swiss-educated pathologist in private practice in New York City. RNA (ribonucleic acid), a molecule in each of our cells, directs the production of the many different kinds of proteins necessary to carry on life. As we grow older, some researchers believe, we gradually lose the ability to make enough quality RNA, and because of this our cells gradually cease to function well. Frank believes there are certain foods that, if ingested in high enough concentrations, can both repair and prevent this RNA breakdown. RNA therapy, as developed by Frank, is designed to get a new and constant supply of RNA into our systems.

"Thousands of aged patients whom I've treated with nucleic acids have enjoyed spectacular improvement," Frank says. "Patients in their eighties and nineties who were suffering from a wide range of complications of aging such as heart disease, arthritis, emphysema, and diabetes felt dramatically better after only a month or two." In fact, he says, older patients appear ten years younger than they did before treatment, and younger patients (thirty to fifty) appear to lose five to ten years of age.

There are three methods of Frank's treatment: dietary, supplemental, and organ-specific.

The dietary regimen consists of increasing the consumption of foods Frank has determined are rich in nucleic acids: sweetbreads, anchovies, sardines, liver, kidneys, and meat extracts, as well as fish.

The supplemental regime consists of eating RNA supplements refined from yeast, which Frank believes will mean a return to vitality, good looks, and stamina. Indeed, in animal experiments with RNA, Frank says, "not only did the activity of these mice increase considerably but their dry and matted hair became softer and their general, obviously old, appearance became more youthful."

The organ-specific diet means taking RNA from an animal organ to treat a human organ. For instance, Frank believes that if we can inject liver RNA into ourselves, our livers will become better—and the same is true with heart RNA or any other organ-specific RNA. This method is more expensive than the other two, and must be supervised by a physician. But in these treatments Frank claims he was able to rejuvenate liver function in 60 percent of the cases he treated.

Frank's concept has several adherents within the scientific community, such as Dr. Sheldon Hendler, professor of biochemistry at the University of California in San Diego. Hendler states that we "probably have a greater need for nucleic acid [RNA] than the cells can make. Dr. Frank is the first to realize this and to propose a diet that contains these vital constituents."

Perhaps Frank has discovered a significant way to combat aging, but aside from the "pinch test," which measures the age related loss of elasticity in the skin, there are few methods of accurately gauging how effective this diet can be. Frank reports an improvement of between 30 and 40 percent after three months of RNA supplement in women forty to seventy-one years old, according to the speed of pinched skin returning to its normal position. But his claims that "Anyone who follows my 'Youth Diet' could lengthen his life span by as much as twenty years and be in good shape all the time he lives" are, to say the least, hard to substantiate. In fact, there are substantial counterarguments to his claims.

As we will see in later chapters, nucleic acid breakdown is thought by some scientists to be related to aging, but it is doubtful these control molecules, which make up less than 2 percent of body's weight, contribute to aging because their *amount* within the body diminishes. Rather, it is more likely that individual cells gradually lose their ability to repair the RNA and DNA—deoxyribonucleic acid, which is related—molecules. Simply increasing the amount of DNA or RNA in the diet will probably not have any effect on the repair mechanisms within the cell.

In addition, DNA and RNA, when ingested, are broken down by the stomach into their constituent chemicals, called nucleotides.

These nucleotides, traveling to the various organs and cells, are simply building blocks of DNA and RNA; they are not the finished chemicals. Thus, if one ingests doses of organ-specific DNA and RNA, as Frank recommends, they will reach the cells in a nonspecific form. If the aging cells can still accurately replenish and replace their worn-out molecules, the ingested DNA and RNA may be helpful. But if the age-related condition of the cells has deteriorated too greatly, then the ingested DNA and RNA will become simply another waste product.

Dr. Frank's work may ultimately prove important. But it cannot, as of now, be assessed as valuable, simply on the amount of data currently available.

Clearly, getting the right food into our bodies is a start toward health and therefore longevity. There are those, however, who believe that by proper diet alone a large number of healthy years can be added to our life spans.

ADELLE DAVIS AND EATING RIGHT

Adelle Davis was perhaps the most popularly known figure in the diet and health field. An international author, a nutritionist and biochemist trained at Purdue, the University of Southern California, and UCLA, and a dietary consultant, she estimated that during her career she personally planned diets for more than 20,000 people suffering from various diseases.

Through television, articles, and books (such as *Let's Eat Right to Keep Fit* and *Let's Cook It Right)* she promoted the idea that nearly all life-shortening diseases—heart attacks, cancer, high blood pressure, and others—were caused by improper diet. "Persons over sixty-five years of age suffer 40 percent of all illness in the United States, yet make up only 8 percent of the population," she stated, "and their diets have been found to be deficient in almost every nutrient except calories." Simple dietary alterations, she claimed, changed oldsters "from semi-invalids into vital individuals who still find life an exciting adventure."

Among her recommendations she stressed eating vitamins from natural sources (for example, Vitamin A from squash, broccoli, carrots, and apricots) and eating plenty of protein from organ meat sources. She also advocated the use of foods in their most natural state—no white, processed flour, no refined sugar. Instead, she recommended cooking with unrefined brown sugar, or honey, and unbleached whole grains. Like other nutritionists, Davis held that dietary loss also resulted from the way foods are prepared; frying and overboiling of foods, she insisted, destroyed food value. Exercises such as swimming and running were also on her list of promoted activities.

Davis felt quite strongly about the effects of her dietary and exercise recommendations. "Unless something is done and done quickly toward real prevention," she stated, "I think we can expect still more irritability, fatigue, mental sluggishness, psychological maladjustment, faulty posture and bone structure, crooked and decayed teeth. We can expect more surgery, more tumors, more cancers, gall bladders and prostates removed, more sinuses scraped, more hysterectomies performed." She also believed that "ulcers, high blood pressure, heart disease, diabetes, muscular dystrophy and atrophy, multiple sclerosis, cerebral palsy" would increase in the future because the American diet was becoming worse and worse.

Although a number of her ideas seem sound, there has been considerable controversy over her claims. When attacked by physicians who believed the American diet is adequate as it stands, Davis responded that few medical schools taught nutrition, and that "if nutrition is taught, it is usually limited to the recognition and treatment of severe deficiencies rather than subtle ones."

Unfortunately, even though Adelle Davis followed all of her own dietary and exercise advice, in 1974 she died at the age of seventy—of cancer, a disease she believed to be caused by improper diet. She was about five and a half years under the national average for age at death of women. Late in life she stated that her cancer was caused by the "junk food" she ate in college—more than forty years before her death.

LINUS PAULING AND VITAMINS FOR LONGEVITY

Dr. Linus Pauling is the figure in the scientific community who has done the most to promote the diet and longevity connection. He is the only person to have twice won the Nobel Prize without sharing the award with others. The first was awarded in 1954, in chemistry, for his research into the way atoms join together to form chemical compounds. The second, which came in 1962, was for peace, and was given for his long-time opposition to nuclear weapons.

In 1965, Pauling became interested in nutrition—his wife is a nutritionist—and he began experiments, primarily on himself, aimed at discovering what quantities of vitamins are needed for optimum health. "I think," he says, "that it is possible that by the proper intake of vitamins and other nutrients, and by refraining from smoking cigarettes, and decreasing the amount of sugar ingested, life may be lengthened by sixteen to twenty-four years."

Pauling practices what he preaches. His own vitamin consumption is very large. He takes 2 grams of Vitamin C, 1,200 units of Vitamin E, 50 milligrams each of several types of B vitamins (thirty times the government's recommended daily allowances), as well as 4,000 units of Vitamin A.

Pauling takes issue with the government's standards for minimum daily vitamin requirements because he feels that they are well below what we need. "If you read their reports carefully," he says, "you find that they have never attempted to find the *optimum* intake of substances that would put people in the best of health."

Pauling's reasoning for taking these tremendous doses of vitamins is that, over the last two million years or so, man evolved in a tropical environment that produced fruits and vegetables with extremely high Vitamin C concentrations. As a result of living in a Vitamin C-rich environment, man gradually lost his ability to manufacture the vitamin within his body. Pauling believes that most people suffer dramatic Vitamin C deficiencies—with many people receiving only 1 or 2 percent of the amount they require for vibrant health. He realizes, however, that there are also other vital nutrients: "The important thing to remember is that nutrients act as a team— you need the whole works, not just one vitamin."

In 1970, Pauling published a highly successful book called *Vitamin C and the Common Cold,* which advocated taking a daily dose of between 250 milligrams and 10 grams of Vitamin C. Pauling did not draw a distinction between taking the expensive natural

Vitamin C, which comes from such sources as rose hips and acerola cherry, and the inexpensive synthetic Vitamin C manufactured in laboratories. Both types, he believes, work equally well.

Although there has been some medical criticism of Pauling's claims, he continues to maintain that the human life span can be extended through the ingestion of large doses of vitamins. Evidence at this time, however, is both incomplete and inconclusive.

THE SEARCH FOR HOMO LONGEVUS

However doubtful the results for some of the unorthodox life-extending procedures, medical and engineering schools and scientific laboratories of international repute are unquestionably making startling advances in youth-prolonging and antiaging techniques.

Lives that only a decade ago would be over are now being extended with organ transplants such as hearts, kidneys, bone marrow, and other parts. And where such parts are unsatisfactory or unavailable, metals, synthetic materials and bionic machines are now commonplace.

Low-temperature strategies may extend life by dropping our bodies' temperatures a few degrees, or by adapting the techniques of hibernating animals. We may even develop techniques for freezing the body against a time when rejuvenation will be a possibility.

Cellular transformation, following several new biological theories of aging, may allow us to forestall or even reverse the aging process.

And the final key, genetic engineering, may well be the one that teaches us how to stop the inner clock.

"We will lick the problem of aging completely," said Augustus Kinzel, former president of the Salk Institute of Biological Studies in La Jolla, California, in 1967, "so that accidents will be essentially the only cause of death."

Let us now consider the first front of the advance against aging—the area of transplants.

4. The Promise of Transplants

There are nearly 867,000 people each year whose lives will end as the result of the breakdown of a single organ and the complications arising from it. One of the ways we are beginning to overcome this cause of death is by surgically transplanting organs from another source.

Louis Washkansky ("Washy" to his friends), owner of a grocery store in Cape Town, South Africa, prided himself on his ability to withstand punishment. During World War II he fought the Germans in Kenya, Egypt, and Italy, and his friends said that it was impossible to get Washy down. It was almost true. In December 1959, he suffered a heart attack—an episode of angina pectoris, a restriction of the flow of blood to the heart muscle, which sometimes results in the death of part of the heart. However, he was able to recover from the attack at home. A year later he had another heart attack, and when the doctor called by his wife ordered him into the hospital, he refused to go. Still he survived. Five years later the angina struck again—and this time the pain was so great that he forced himself to drive to the nearest hospital.

The Cape Town doctors found that Washkansky's previous attacks had badly damaged his heart, and as a result the general state of his health was also extremely poor: he had diabetes, his lungs were congested, he had failing kidneys, and water had begun to accumulate in his tissues.

By 1966, at age fifty-two, he was in great pain. His legs were swollen with excess fluids, his kidneys worked poorly, his lungs were bleeding, his heart was swollen and pumping at only a sixth of its normal capacity. Hospitalized for long periods of time, he occasionally became delerious. At that point, Dr. Christiaan Barnard was brought in on the case.

Without ever having examined Washkansky, Barnard knew, from the results of hospital tests, that the patient did not have long to live. Barnard then mentioned to Washkansky the possibility of a highly experimental procedure—transplanting someone else's heart into his body. Washkansky, knowing the risks, agreed to the operation.

On December 2, 1967, Denise Darval, twenty-five, a bank clerk, lost control of her car and collided with another one. Brought to the hospital, it was apparent she was near death. Barnard had her tissues tested to see if they were compatible with Washkansky's, and then approached her parents for permission to transplant her heart if she died. Within minutes of her death, her heart was removed and Washkansky was prepared for surgery and anesthetized. Barnard made an incision in his chest, connected up a heart-lung machine to take over the vital functions, and removed the damaged heart. He then connected Denise Darval's twenty-five-year-old heart to Washkansky's fifty-three-year-old body.

Washkansky lived for nearly a month, to the surprise of many doctors. One eminent pathologist, Jan Van Rood of Holland, had said "If Washkansky lives for more than five days, it would be a major step forward in 'spare part' surgery." An autopsy showed that the heart looked healthy and normal. There was only slight inflammation—a swelling of the heart owing to the aftereffects of surgery, similar to the inflammation seen around a healing cut. In fact, Washkansky did not die of heart failure. He died of pneumonia as a result of the drugs Barnard had used to prevent Washkansky's body from rejecting the foreign heart tissue.

We have come a long way in organ transplantation since that 1967 operation. Today the kidneys of a person who has perished in a car accident may six hours later be helping another person live. Through computer networks of donor-recipient tissue matching, such as that of the U.S. Army's Walter Reed Organ Donor and Transport Program, based in Washington, D.C., people are living longer now who less than ten years ago would have had absolutely no chance of survival.

The idea of transplanting organs from one person to another is not new. The ancient Egyptian medical text, the Ebers Papyrus, written about 1500 B.C., contains a reference to skin grafting, where skin is relocated from one part of the body to another for the purpose of covering an open wound, disfigurement, or scar. The Hindu Vedas also describe skin transplant operations. The ancient Indians prepared the skin donation site, such as the buttocks, by beating the tissue with a wooden paddle until the skin was red and swollen. Over the wound that would receive the graft they placed a leaf that was then cut to match this part of the body. This leaf "stencil" was next placed over the beaten area and a layer of skin was painfully peeled off the body and placed over the wound site. The donated skin was held in place, until it fused to the recipient site, with a "secret cement"—the formula of which was not given in the Hindu texts.

The great Roman surgeon Celsus, who lived around the time of Christ, wrote about transplanting tissues from one part of the body to another. He stated with firm conviction that such transplants would survive quite well in their new sites. And in the third century A.D., two Arab physicians, brothers named Cosmas and Damian, who were later proclaimed saints, supposedly removed the gangrenous leg of a Roman and replaced it with a healthy leg taken from a slave. The operation is depicted in a 500-year-old wood carving at the Cathedral of Valencia in Spain, and the cathedral records describe the operation in detail. A painting done in the fifteenth century shows the two saints removing the leg from a boy and replacing it with another leg. It is not known whether the transplants really worked, although Dr. José Rivas Torres, a medical professor at

Spain's Malaga University, believes the Valencia wood carving is historical evidence that medicine was "fantastically advanced centuries ago." On such matters opinions vary widely.

After the Roman era, however, the idea of transplantation disappeared, as a result of the early Church's prohibition against dissection, surgery, and medicine. The reason for banning the practice of medicine, the Church fathers said, was that "the Church abhors the shedding of blood." All studies of anatomy were suspended and medical progress halted for several hundred years. It was not until the Renaissance, for example, that the first recorded autopsies were performed (some of the first by the great Leonardo da Vinci). The transplanting of organs did not become a real surgical possibility until the late 1800s. And one man, Alexis Carrel, almost singlehandedly made the procedure possible.

ALEXIS CARREL AND THE NEW SURGERY

In June 1894 the President of France, Sadi Carnot, was stabbed by an Italian anarchist while addressing a crowd during a political rally in Lyon. The knife severed Carnot's portal vein, the major blood vessel carrying blood to the liver. No surgeon at that time thought that such a massive break in a major blood vessel could be surgically repaired; thus, no attempt was made to save Carnot's life, and he died of internal bleeding. His body was brought to the Red Cross Hospital in Lyon where Alexis Carrel was then a young intern. After seeing the body, Carrel insisted that the president's life could have been saved, asserting that blood vessels could be sutured together in a manner similar to that done in closing a wound.

In those days there was difficulty in suturing the two ends of a severed artery or vein because the tissue composing the walls of blood vessels was soft and slippery and was capable of holding its shape only when filled with blood. The sutures also often proved too weak to hold the ends of the vessels together when they filled with blood, and many times an injured vessel would suddenly burst apart, causing massive internal bleeding. Moreover, the type of surgical thread then available was made primarily of cotton, which was often an irritant to the blood and caused it to clot. A blood clot could make its way to the brain or lungs and produce blood stoppage—called an embolism—in the lungs or a stroke in the brain. Both were often fatal. In addition, the manner in which doctors then used surgical clamps on blood vessels often damaged the fragile vessel walls, causing irregularities around which blood clots would form, stopping the flow of blood.

With great energy Carrel threw himself into a program of research designed to produce a surgical technique capable of re-uniting severed arteries and veins, and made considerable progress in a short time. At the same time he began to vent some wildly reactionary ideas on white supremacy, calling for the extermination of all "inferior" peoples and trying to promote an almost feudalistic type of politics. He also told of witnessing a "miracle" at the religious shrine at Lourdes. Having already failed twice on his exam to become a surgeon, he was told that his eccentric views would make it impossible for the medical examiners to pass him the third time. Seeing no future in France, Carrel went to Canada in 1904, where he gave a paper at a Medical Congress in Montreal on his research in blood vessel surgery. He so impressed an American surgeon attending the conference that he was later offered a position at the University of Chicago, which he accepted. Finally, toward the end of 1905 he announced that he had perfected a method of rejoining severed blood vessels—the first such completely successful technique ever devised.

As Charles Hufnagel, a heart surgeon at Georgetown University, described it, Carrel's basic method required that "three sutures be placed equidistant on the circumference of the divided (separated) artery, approximately 120 degrees apart. By applying traction to two of the three sutures, he converted one-third of the circumference to a straight line, and by sewing each of the segments and rotating the sutures, he united the artery." During World War I this technique alone enabled army field surgeons to save the lives of thousands of what would otherwise have been mortally wounded soldiers. Today it permits surgeons to join together the blood vessels from a donated kidney to those in the body of a transplant recipient. For this contribution, and his perfecting of a method of sterilizing wounds, Carrel was awarded the 1912 Nobel Prize in medicine. In 1921, he was awarded the U.S. Army's Distinguished Service Medal for his part in "the saving of many lives and limbs and the prevention of many disabilities among the wounded." A unique and inventive genius, Carrell is intimately tied to the progress made in twentieth-century medicine. Once the suturing of blood vessels was mastered, the other surgical techniques needed to implant organs were not extremely exotic or difficult. Thus, almost alone, Alexis Carrel made modern surgery and the transplantation of human organs possible.

Being insatiably curious Carrel collected around him brilliant and gifted people. Some of them shared his mystical views about the superiority of the white race, some of them, in fact, revered the Nazi state then emerging in Germany. One man who became a close friend was the aviator Charles Lindbergh.

In 1929 Carrel began experimenting with trying to create a culture medium, a bloodlike solution that could provide cells with nutrients and oxygen after being removed from the body. To complete the project he realized he needed a "perfusion pump" that would flood the isolated cells with the culture medium to keep them alive. Lindbergh agreed to help design such a pump. Carrel's objective was to take isolated heart cells, for example, and keep them alive and growing outside of the body, hoping these isolated cells would reproduce the entire organ from which they were taken, and that such an artificially grown organ could then be used to replace a diseased and weak organ.

For six years Carrel and Lindbergh worked at building their perfusion pump and finally created an apparatus made of glass and powered by air pressure that could sustain cells with nourishment outside the body and also, for short periods of time, keep entire organs alive after their removal from a body. Although they never succeeded in producing an artificially grown heart from isolated cells (despite the fact that a 1935 *Time* magazine cover story announced they had), their pump served to kindle interest in two new fields— the transplantation of human organs and the creation of artificial bionic organ replacements. But it was not until twelve years later that transplant operations became a reality.

DAVID HUME AND THE FIRST
KIDNEY TRANSPLANT

When David Hume, a fast-talking, high-energy graduate of Harvard Medical School, got out of the Navy after World War II, he began work at Peter Bent Brigham Hospital in Boston as a very unusual specialist: a surgeon who could skillfully connect people to artificial kidney machines causing as little damage to their arteries as possible. In those days,* kidney machines, developed in Holland during the war, were still very experimental and it was impossible to connect someone to a machine more than a few times in a several month period. The problem was not with the machine but with the patient's arteries, which fed blood into the machine. These arteries had to be surgically punctured each time the machine was used. There were no implantable shunts and valves, as there are now, to turn a single artery into a permanent connection for the machine, and each time the machine was hooked up to a person an artery was damaged.

An endocrinologist as well as a surgeon, Hume watched with frustration as patients suffering from kidney failure were brought in to use the machine. He knew that if their kidney damage was irreparable, the machine would at best prolong their lives only a few months, because eventually damage to the arteries would be too great. As a result, he and others on the team of kidney specialists began considering the feasibility of transplanting kidneys from people who had recently died into patients who had lost the function of their own organs. For months, Hume practiced transplanting the kidneys of dogs, learning how to suture the arteries and how to transplant a kidney into the body cavity. Because their bodies' immune systems, which have the function of resisting harmful bacteria and viruses, eventually rejected the transplanted kidneys, none of the dogs lived for long; but Hume continued to perfect the surgical technique.

Since the technique was experimental and there was no way of knowing what problems might develop in humans, it was decided the first transplant should be tried on a person who would need the donated organ only for a short time, until his own kidneys healed. In

1947 just such a patient, a young woman with kidneys severely damaged by an infection caught during pregnancy, was brought to the hospital. A suitable donor organ was obtained from another patient who had died, and Hume began the operation—carrying out the procedure in a small room by the light of two small lamps, since the patient was so ill that even moving her to an operating room might have cost too much time.

The kidney was not implanted directly into the patient's body. Rather, while the organ rested on her arm covered with wet sponges, Hume simply connected the woman to the kidney via one of the main arteries in her arm. For three days the woman's blood was circulated through the kidney, feeding it with nutrients; the kidney in turn filtered the blood of impurities. By the fourth day the kidney had begun to fail, but by then the woman's own kidneys had begun to function again. With this operation, modern transplantation became possible.

After 1949, Hume began experimenting with placing the kidney inside the patient's body. At first the donated organ was placed inside the lower abdomen, with the ureter (the tube that carries urine) going not into the bladder but extending through a hole in the skin. However, since the exposed ureter allowed the kidney to become easily infected, none of the early recipients lived more than seven months. Then Hume placed the transplanted kidneys nearer to their natural anatomical site and connected the ureters to the bladders of the recipients, so that the excretion of urine was more or less natural. But except for organs transplanted between relatives, the success rate was still not impressive.

It became apparent that a transplant operation where the kidney was donated by a father to his son had a much greater chance for success than a transplant from nonblood relatives. In fact, at first transplants between unrelated people had a zero success rate. Conversely, the transplant of a kidney from one identical twin to another had the greatest chance of success. Indeed, the first successful human kidney transplant was between twins in 1954—and the boy receiving the kidney survived for another eighteen years.

The reason for the lack of success with nonrelatives was that the recipient's body rejected the foreign organ as if it were an invading, life-threatening bacteria. The transplants were failures precisely because the human immune system was so successful. As we will see, a great deal of research has gone into trying to overcome this rejection problem.

A TRANSPLANT INVENTORY: WHERE WE STAND NOW

In 1969, Dr. Robert Schwartz of New England Center Hospital in Boston, observed that "Just a decade ago, organ transplants were considered impossible by knowledgeable scientists, except for an impassioned minority." There are now almost 7,000 people still alive after kidney transplants because of that "impassioned minority."

Kidney operations are the most successful of the organ transplants, but headway is also being made in other areas. Here is a run-down of the status of the various kinds of operations.

Heart

Since Louis Washkansky was operated on in Cape Town, heart transplantation—the most dramatic of the transplant operations—has come a long way. As of December 1975, 286 heart transplants had been performed by sixty-four teams of surgeons all over the world. Fifty of these patients are still alive. The longest survivor, a fifty-six-year-old Wisconsin housewife, received her new heart in 1967.

Hearts offer many surgical problems, as well as rejection problems. Each day the heart beats about 100,000 times and pumps about 2,000 gallons of blood through the body. Its four valves each open and close about 400,000 times a day, forcing blood through 60,000 miles of blood vessels. With this kind of physical exertion, surgical procedure must be perfect for the heart to work. From this purely technical point of view, heart transplant surgery is extremely difficult, yet it is usually rejection and disease that causes this operation to fail.

Today only a few centers are still transplanting hearts, because of the generally experimental nature of the operation. The most active is Stanford University, where a team headed by Dr. Norman Shumway performs about one heart transplant a month, and has a success rate well above the worldwide average.

Kidneys

As of August 1975 there have been 16,444 kidney transplants at 288 centers all over the world. In follow-up studies of 14,479 of these patients, it was found that 47 percent were alive with kidney function, 21 percent were alive without kidney function and had to rely on dialysis machines, and 32 percent had died. (Close to two-thirds of those who died had full kidney function at death; they succumbed because of disease, accident, or surgical failure.)

Survival of patients for at least five years, is about 71 percent if the transplant is from a sibling, 62 percent if from a parent, and about 50 percent if from a cadaver. There have been fifty-five cases of women with kidney transplants getting pregnant and successfully delivering a baby.

Every year the overall kidney statistics get better. As Lt. Colonel Jimmy A. Light, M.D., Assistant Chief of the Walter Reed Organ Transplant Program, states, "with optimum donor-recipient selection, as many as 80 percent of these transplants can be successful for over five years."

Liver

As of April 1974 there were 200 liver transplants, with eleven surviving for over one year but only one surviving for five years. The problem is that a breakdown in liver function pollutes the bloodstream with waste products and toxins, and this in turn weakens every cell in the body. With liver disorders, unlike with kidney disorders, there is no machine available as a temporary replacement, so that the general health in people with liver dysfunction cannot be maintained.

The chances of success will be better when a way is found to maintain a person with a diseased or damaged liver in good health until a replacement organ is located. Even so, as Thomas E. Starzl of the University of Colorado—the first surgeon to transplant a liver—says, "liver transplantation is now a feasible and legitimate, albeit imperfect, form of treatment."

Pancreas

The pancreas controls the secretion of insulin, which in turn controls the body's use of sugar. Because a patient with a defective pancreas can still receive insulin by mouth or by injection, the pancreas transplant is therefore rarely the only means available to save a patient's life. Even so, there have been forty-six pancreas transplants, the first one in December 1966 by Dr. Richard C. Lillihei at the University of Minnesota Medical School.

Two recipients survived almost two years, and the rest either lost function in their transplant as a consequence of rejection or died a short time after the operation. However, one person is still alive, four years after his transplant.

Cornea

There have been over 4,000 cornea transplants in centers all over the United States and it is used for the treatment of blindness caused by corneal scarring. The transplantation of this clear outermost layer of the eye is completely successful about 25 percent of the time. More commonly, however, the surgeon makes only a partial graft, transplanting some of the many layers of the cornea onto the recipient's eye, and the success rate for this operation is extremely high, nearly 95 percent.

But corneas do not offer the same problems as do other organs because they have no blood supply and therefore are not exposed to the immune cells in the bloodstream. The high failure rate for the full transplant operation is a result of surgical difficulties.

Bones

The first fifteen operations for bone transplants were done in 1974, and since then there have been eight more. The operations directed by Dr. Henry J. Mankin, chief of orthopedic surgery at Massachusetts General Hospital in Boston, gave fifteen cancer patients bones from the newly dead, thus avoiding the necessity for amputation of arms and legs that would otherwise have had to be removed. All but three of the patients had relatively free use of their limbs within a few months of surgery.

In recent years, research uncovered the fact that patients' immune systems would accept the bone transplants if the bones were first frozen and then thawed.

Umbilical Cords

Polyester blood vessels often work well in heart by-pass operations but not for long in legs and feet as replacement veins for patients suffering from vascular disease. Twin brothers in New Jersey, Irving and Herbert Dardik, both vascular surgeons, came up with a series of chemical pretreatments by which to shape, size, and preserve human umbilical cord veins and arteries as "biografts." The Dardiks grafted these vessels into more than thirty patients who faced death or amputation of feet or legs for lack of suitable grafting material.

Lungs

Since 1963, thirty-eight experimental lung transplants have been tried. There are no survivors at present. Only three patients lasted longer than a month. The principal reason for lack of success is that lungs are particularly difficult to store, once removed from the body. The thousands of miles of tiny capillaries inside the organ make it hard to wash the lung clean of blood, and the result is that many of the tiny air sacs that function in taking in oxygen become filled with blood clots.

Another difficulty is that the lung must start working as soon as it is implanted. A kidney implanted into a person can rest passively as long as that person is hooked up to an artificial kidney machine. But a transplanted lung must start functioning immediately, because without oxygen the body will die in minutes. There are also surgical difficulties in suturing the airways so as to prevent their pulling apart or closing from blood clots.

Still, Dr. Frank J. Veith, of Montefiore Hospital in New York City, who has done lung transplantation, is optimistic. "Despite the somewhat disappointing human experience to date," he states, "and despite the large number of complex problems that must be over-come, the prospects are excellent that increasing success with human lung transplantation will be achieved."

The Nervous System

In 1957, Vladimer Demikov, a Russian surgeon, performed an incredible experiment: he transplanted the head of one dog onto the body of another, producing a two-headed animal. For five days the animal lived, and though weak, was able to stand on its own. When exposed to light and sound, both heads responded by trying to bark. Movies showed the animal with Demikov pointing out the place where the second head was grafted to the body, and where the arteries and veins were connected. When both host animal and transplanted head died, it was as a result of a massive immune response. This kind of "brain transplant" is such science-fiction stuff, however, that American scientists have been extremely dubious as to its viability.

A more believable line of research was demonstrated many years later, in June 1976, at a Florida conference of neuroscientists. There another Russian, Dr. Levon A. Matinian, showed motion pictures of rats that had regained a remarkable degree of movement after having had their spinal cords severed and then treated with enzyme injections. And he stated that those rats that did recover regained complete use of their hind legs within two to eight months. Although American scientists have still been critical of the Russians' scientific methods, there seems to be every indication that the hitherto widespread conviction in this country that central nervous system regeneration is impossible is about to be reversed. To scientists who see new vistas opening, this offers exciting possibilities. While it may be years before the knowledge can be applied, eventually nerve regeneration will be able to help paraplegics, stroke victims, and others suffering from damage to brain and spinal cord.

For effective regeneration to take place, the neurons that were once connected and are now severed must be kept alive, for there is no possibility of reconnecting dead cells. The neuron must also grow its axon—the appendage that transmits impulses—far enough to connect with the next neuron. It cannot grow in the wrong direction or be blocked by scar tissues.

The Russians have used enzyme therapy on humans with spinal injuries and, although they refuse to divulge details or success rates, claim to have achieved "a positive effect." The purpose of the enzymes—there are two used in combination, known as trypsin and hyaluronidase—is to prevent the formation of scar tissue, which may hinder growing nerve fiber, and to break down dead nerve tissue and make available more cellular material for the growth of new nerve tissues. The Russians stress that the enzymes are most successful when given immediately after an accident, and don't work at all when spinal cord damage is extremely severe.

DETECTIVE STORY: TRYING TO OVERCOME TRANSPLANT REJECTION

As we indicated earlier, the greatest problem in organ transplants is that the recipient's body will reject the donated organ.

Usually rejection of a transplant occurs in episodes. At first the danger of the transplanted organ's being completely destroyed is great, then there is a respite, then several months later the immune system may launch a very active attack against the transplant. The first episode usually comes within a few days after the operation, the most dangerous time because the patient is usually very weak from the trauma of the operation and from the effects of the disease or injury that made the transplant necessary. If a patient manages to survive the first episode, he will probably be able to leave the hospital and resume a relatively normal existence until the onset of the next rejection episode. Eventually, the transplanted organ will again be subjected to a massive attack by the immune system and probably cease functioning. By that time, the patient, weakened by the loss of the vital functions of the transplanted organ, will probably die.

This is the natural course of an organ transplant operation if nothing is done to prevent rejection. Researchers and surgeons realized, when they began to experiment with transplants, that they had to do something to suppress the immune system's rejection

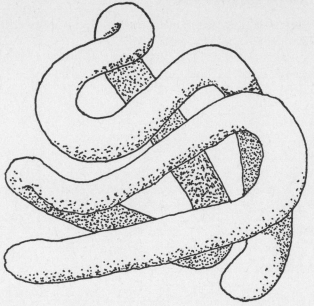

A typical protein. The long chain of atoms (amino acids) is folded into an intricate shape that allows the protein to perform its function inside the cell.

reaction if they were to successfully transplant any organ. To understand how they attacked this, we must describe how the immune system works.

The immune system is a group of organs and cells whose function is to fight off harmful bacteria, viruses, and cancer, as well as to reject foreign tissue such as transplants. The key to the immune system is the body's ability to recognize proteins that are foreign to it. Proteins are long, folded chains of atoms (see illustration) which serve as the basic building blocks of our bodies and which direct most of the chemical reactions that occur in our cells. Most of the human body—skin, hair, muscles, fingernails, organs—is composed of protein. The instructions that enable cells to make these many different kinds of proteins needed for growth and normal replacement are stored in the nucleus of each cell. The instructions are composed of chains of molecules called DNA (short for deoxyribonucleic acid—see the illustration). This DNA code, which we inherit from our parents, dictates what kinds of proteins our cells will produce. Many of the proteins specified by the DNA instructions are the same in all of us, especially those that direct our basic life

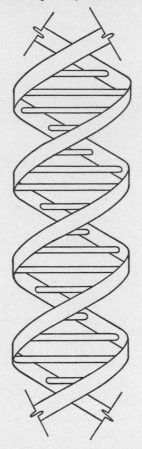

Structure of DNA. Known as a "double helix" because the molecule consists of two strands, each strand made of billions of precisely ordered atoms coiled around each other, this molecule contains the inherited instruction code that is in each of our cells and that states what kind of cell it is going to be—for example, liver, thyroid, blood.

processes, such as hemoglobin, which is in our red blood cells and carries oxygen to all body cells. Other proteins are unique to each of us, so that a biochemist examining those proteins could distinguish between individuals just as a detective can distinguish people by their fingerprints. The only people who have identical proteins of *everything* are identical twins, because they both have inherited identical DNA instructions. Identical twins, who look alike (fraternal twins do not), will accept transplants from one another without problems; the rest of us have varying degrees of difficulty, depending on how closely our tissues match those of the donor.

How does the immune system recognize our special proteins? Our unique proteins are found on the membranes of each of our billions of cells. The membrane surrounds each cell like a skin and regulates the intake of nutrients and other chemicals into the cell and the excretion of waste materials by the cell. These surface proteins (called transplantation proteins, because of the role they play in transplants)—act as keys which can fit two kinds of locks in the immune system—the T and B cells. (T stands for the thymus, the small gland under the breastbone and the production site for T cells. B stands for the bursa of Fabricius, an intestinal organ in the chicken; the production site of B cells in humans is still unknown.) The T and B cell locks will accept only the keys of each person's own unique surface proteins.

If bacteria or viruses (or transplants, which are composed of foreign protein) enter the body, their surface-protein keys will not fit the T and B locks. This mismatch provokes the T and B cells into a defensive reaction. The T cells become killers, attacking and destroying the foreign organisms. The B cells release antibodies, special proteins that "tag" or identify the foreign organisms and thereby attract a special immune cell (called a macrophage, or "big eater") that gobbles up the invaders. The tagging process itself may also weaken the membranes around an invading cell and cause it to burst apart. This immune response has protected us for millions of years, and is a difficult system to short-circuit—even for the life-sustaining purpose of organ transplantation.

Occasionally, the T and B cells go haywire and attack the body's own cells as if they were covered with foreign protein. This inability to distinguish between foreign and "self" cells is called an *autoimmune* disease, because the body attacks itself. Examples are arthritis and myasthenia gravis (degeneration of the nerves controlling the muscles). The great Australian medical researcher Sir Frank MacFarlane Burnet, describes autoimmune disease as something like "a mutiny in the security forces of a country." Sometimes the opposite of an autoimmune disease happens and the immune system does not attack the invaders. This loss of defensive function is called *tolerance:* the immune system "tolerates" the presence of foreign organisms.

Normally, Burnet theorized, the immune system learns, during development in the mother's uterus, to tolerate only its own cells and to attack all others. But before this "learning" process took place, Burnet felt, a human immune system would tolerate *any* protein. Thus, autoimmune disease occurred when immune cells "forgot" the self-recognition ability they had learned during development. Burnet's theory was confirmed experimentally by Sir Peter Medawar of University College, London, in 1953. Medawar operated on pregnant mice and exposed their fetuses. He then carefully injected each fetus with cells from an adult mouse. After the mice he had operated on were born, Medawar discovered that they would tolerate skin transplants from the adult mice that donated the cells used to inject them. The injected mice had become tolerant to the foreign cells because the cells were there when the "learning" process of the immune system took place, and the immune system therefore considered the injected cells to be normal body cells. Medawar termed this experimental production of tolerance "acquired tolerance."

The implications of this experiment were far-reaching. As Burnet says, "Once it had been shown that a mouse could be persuaded to retain a graft of foreign tissue . . . the possibility of applying the idea to allow transplantation of tissues or organs between human beings was evident to everyone." But while this line of investigation was being pursued, scientists were trying to cope in a variety of ways with the immediate problems of overcoming the rejection reaction.

Killing by X-Ray

During the 1950s the only method of immunosuppression—the medical name for preventing the rejection response—was to destroy the patient's T and B cells by irradiating the entire body with X-rays. This technique allowed a transplant to be accepted for longer periods of time.

Unfortunately, since the immune system's main job is to protect our bodies from infection by bacteria and viruses, destroying the T and B cells removed all that disease protection. Thus, when Dr. John P. Merrill, a colleague of David Hume at Brigham Hospital in Boston, was faced in April 1958 with a woman who had no kidneys (and no identical twin), he was forced to try, for the first time on a human being, suppressing the rejection response with whole body irradiation. To prevent infection afterwards, the woman was kept in a sterile operating room for a month. Everything the patient was surrounded by and came into contact with had to be sterilized—her bedclothes, the clothes of everyone entering the room, the whole operating room, as well as all the equipment used in the irradiation and the subsequent kidney transplant.

The transplant itself was a success, and shortly after the operation the kidney produced normal urine. However, the damage to the woman from the irradiation was too great, and she died thirty-two days later with infection spreading through her system. (People treated with such irradiation can become infected with virus, bacteria, and fungus, which normally are easily defeated by the body's defenses.) Other transplant teams throughout the world continued to use whole body irradiation simply because no other method was available. While there were some successes, these transplant recipients usually did not survive for more than a year after the operation. Gradually researchers began to look for less drastic methods of immunosuppression. The most promising was an anticancer drug called mercaptopurine.

Cancer Therapy for Transplants

The cells of the immune system, because they wander through the body's tissues and bloodstream, wear out faster than most other types of cells and must be constantly replaced by new cells. This comes about by cell division, in which one cell divides into two cells. Because production (division) of immune cells is so rapid, they are especially sensitive to that class of drugs whose job it is to attack dividing cells. Cancer cells also divide rapidly, and one main line of cancer therapy has been concerned with the development of drugs such as mercaptopurine, which will kill these rapidly dividing cells.

Animal research showed that whereas irradiation killed T and B cells and destroyed their production sites as well, the cancer drugs killed only the cells. Tests by Dr. David Hume, who had moved to the Medical College of Virginia, showed that use of mercaptopurine could prolong kidney transplants in dogs as much as six times longer than in untreated animals. But a problem with the drug was that infection and side reactions were still present. This was partially overcome in 1960 by chemists who produced a drug similar to mercaptopurine but less toxic called Imuran (or azathioprine).

Very quickly Mercaptopurine and Imuran began to be used experimentally on human kidney transplant patients—mercaptopurine in April 1960 and Imuran in March 1961, both on patients at Boston's Brigham Hospital. Although these two experiments failed because the doctors had not yet found the correct way to use the drugs, a young man operated on in April 1962 by Dr. Joseph Murray of Brigham survived with a new kidney for twenty-one months. Moreover, he survived through a bout of pneumonia and a case of appendicitis, and most of that time was able to live at home and to work. At the end of that period, when the kidney finally failed, he was given a second transplant. A new era had begun in transplanting.

Stalling with Steroids

Although Imuran remains at the center of immunosuppressive treatment, other drugs called corticosteroids (or steroids for short) have also been developed which have similar effects. These are synthetic copies of the steroid hormones produced in the outer layer of the adrenal gland, which lies just above the kidney. These hormones regulate a lot of basic body functions, such as water and salts balance in the tissues. People given steroids often have a characteristic moon-faced look from the accumulation of excess water in their tissues.

Generally, steroids are used to supplement Imuran when a rejection episode occurs. The combination of Imuran and steroids have proved to be a powerful tool in fighting rejection. Some people receiving kidneys from unrelated donors have survived with trans-

planted kidneys for over ten years—an increase in transplant life span
of over 1,200 percent since the early 1950s.

Still, the problem with Imuran and steroids is that they lower
the body's ability to fight disease, as a consequence of which
transplant recipients seem more likely than the average person to get
cancer. Most people, it is believed, produce cancer cells from time to
time but do not get cancer because their immune systems destroy
these cells as soon as they are produced. A breakdown of the
immune system, or a purposeful suppression of the system, may
allow the cancer cells to grow and form tumors.

ALS for All

Another method for suppressing rejection is treatment with a
substance called ALS (for antilymphocyte serum). ALS is designed
not to destroy the T and B cell production sites, as irradiation does,
but to temporarily short-circuit the T and B cell functions.

In 1963, Sir Michael Woodruff, professor of surgery at the
University of Edinburgh, discovered that when he injected T and B
cells from rats into rabbits, the rabbits' bodies, perceiving a foreign
invasion, quickly manufactured specific antibodies to destroy the rat
cells. Then Woodruff removed some blood from the rabbits containing these rat cell-destroying antibodies—called ALS—and administered it *back* into the rats. He next transplanted some foreign skin
to the rats. The result: ALS greatly suppressed the rejection response
of the rats by killing specific T and B cells, and allowed the
transplanted skin to remain for up to twelve times longer than it did
in rats not treated with ALS.

In 1967, after ALS had been tried in a good deal of animal
research, Dr. Thomas Starzl of the University of Chicago tried the
substance on human kidney transplant patients. The result was these
patients survived longer and had fewer and less severe rejection
episodes than did kidney transplant patients treated with conventional immunosuppression. Other physicians tried ALS on patients
receiving transplanted livers and hearts and the results have been
encouraging, especially when used as a supplement rather than as a
replacement for Imuran and steroids.

Still, there have been at least two serious drawbacks to ALS.

For one thing, it is hard to manufacture consistent-strength ALS. Also, ALS increases the chance of getting cancer. Thus, researchers have continued to search for ways to counteract the rejection response. One of these avenues is desensitization.

Desensitization

Desensitization, an extension of Medawar's earlier work in acquired tolerance, is a process borrowed in part from allergy treatments. Allergic reactions are similar to tissue rejection responses. A foreign protein, such as cat hair or pollen, sets up a mild rejection response in the sensitive membranes lining the eyes, nose, and throat, causing sneezing and runny eyes and nose, and irritation of these membranes.

Many allergies are treated with injections of tiny amounts of the offending foreign protein. Sometimes after several treatments, the body becomes desensitized: the small amounts of protein no longer seem to elicit the allergic overreaction, although no one is quite sure how desensitization actually works.

It has been known since the work of Medawar that injecting foreign proteins into a fetus will enable that fetus, when it is born, to later tolerate a skin transplant, for example, from the protein donor. But it was generally agreed that humans, after birth, can no longer be desensitized to foreign proteins, at least not to the transplantation proteins carried on the cells of an organ transplant.

Animals, however, can be desensitized. Foreign proteins taken from cows (purified serum) have been injected in tiny amounts into the bodies of adult rabbits. At first the response of the rabbits is to eliminate foreign cow protein, but after twelve days of continued injections the rabbits show a marked decline in the elimination of the cow protein; they have become slightly desensitized.

Researchers have tried different schedules for administering the foreign protein and different methods for altering the proteins to make them more effective in desensitizing the immune system's response, but so far desensitization is only a hope for use in human beings. Two problems must be overcome. First, for desensitization to be successful in animals, the animal must be exposed to the foreign proteins for long periods of time. But with human transplants, this is often impossible, because the organ, coming from a cadaver, must be used immediately. Second, the animal experiments have so far used only very pure types of proteins. But when an organ is transplanted, surgeons are placing hundreds of different types of proteins into another person's body and it may not be as easy to desensitize so many. Still, desensitization provides a hope of suppressing a rejection response in humans without interfering with other immunological defenses.

Finding Your Type

The need for immunosuppression can be reduced through two techniques that allow doctors to tell in advance of a transplant how severe a rejection response can be expected in a particular patient. One, the mixed lymphocyte test, involves testing the reaction of a recipient's immune cells against cells from his potential donor. Unfortunately, this may take up to seven days to show results, and the need to transplant an organ to save a patient's life may not permit that kind of time.

The second test involves "typing" the cells of both donor and recipient, in much the same way as red blood cells are typed for blood groups before transfusions. Here the results can be known very quickly—in an hour. However, the drawback is that testing solutions are not available for all kinds of typing, so that not everyone can be completely typed. Moreover there is still a possibility of some mismatching which will cause a rejection response that can eventually destroy a transplanted organ.

Still, these tests for compatability—close match of transplantation proteins—have allowed surgeons to achieve much more success with transplants than before, making it possible to use less immunosuppressive treatment, and thus reducing the chance that a transplant patient will get an infection or cancer because his immune defenses are suppressed too greatly.

ORGAN STORAGE AND SOURCES: FROZEN ORGANS AND NEOMORTS

In addition to the immunological problems inherent in the transplantation of organs, there is a great problem of organ availability. Though many people have voluntarily chosen to donate organs to others at the time of their death, there are still too few organs available for those in need. Sometimes an organ may become available but a prospective recipient may be fighting an infection and not able to accept the transplant. The "shelf life" of organs is not indefinite, and a situation can occur where an organ is needed yet decomposes too quickly during the waiting time to be used.

One line of research has been concerned with freezing tissues and organs so that they will be available whenever needed. In 1948 Dr. Audrey U. Smith, at the National Institute for Medical Research in London, accidentally discovered that the chemical *glycerol*, an oily liquid that is a byproduct in the manufacture of soap, protected animal sperm from ice crystal formation—that is, it was an antifreeze agent. This led to attempts at glycerol protection of human sperm, perfected in the early 1960s by Dr. Jerome Sherman of the University of Arkansas, who says there have been over 500 births resulting from artificial insemination with frozen sperm—in two cases, with sperm frozen for over ten years.

These developments stimulated other researchers to try to freeze blood. Ever since blood transfusions became a life-saving technique at the beginning of this century, doctors have been hampered by the "twenty-one-day tyranny," for it is an absolute certainty that refrigerated blood must be discarded after three weeks because of the decay of blood cells. Every day hundreds of pints of old blood are discarded by hospitals and blood banks all over the world. However, in the 1960s, a freezing method (which utilized small amounts of glycerol to protect blood from freezing damage) was developed by Dr. Arthur W. Rowe of the New York Blood Center. Rowe's technique was combined with a method (which used larger amounts of glycerol) devised by Dr. Harold T. Meryman of the American Red Cross. The resulting frozen blood came in time to allow its widespread use during the Vietnam war, and it will be only a matter of time before it becomes an integral part of every civilian blood bank. Among other uses, frozen blood would permit self-donation of blood, against the day a person (especially one with a rare blood type) might need a transfusion.

Blood and sperm are not the only cells or tissues to be successfully frozen for medical use. Frozen bone marrow has been available for use in transplants since 1955, although the method has not been extensively used since fresh cells are usually relatively easy to obtain. Frozen corneas have been in use since the early 1960s, but also have not been used much because the freezing process involves expensive equipment and scarce technical help. Still, research into perfecting the method continues.

The really urgent need at present is to find a way to successfully preserve organs for transplant by freezing. Some progress has been made. Dr. Gerald Moss of the University of Manchester in England has shown that animal livers stored for as long as two weeks at temperatures as low as 80 degrees below zero are capable of metabolic activity when thawed. However, he was unable to successfully transplant these thawed livers. Ronald H. Dietzman, of the University of Minnesota, froze dog kidneys at about the temperature of dry ice (minus 95 degrees) for short periods (less than an hour) and thawed them and successfully transplanted them. The thawed transplanted kidneys functioned as long as a week. Other organs that have been frozen and transplanted, although with limited success, include the heart and pancreas of dogs. The brains of cats and monkeys have been frozen for as long as seven years, and have shown some electrical activity when thawed, according to Dr. Isamu Suda of Kobe Medical College in Japan; thus, even nerve cells of the brain can apparently survive and be revived after long-term storage by freezing. But a considerable amount of research needs to be done before organ preservation for transplants by freezing becomes a reality.

A really startling idea for providing a source of organs for transplantation has been proposed by Willard Gaylin, a psychiatrist and president of the Institute of Society, Ethics, and the Life Sciences in Hastings-on-Hudson, New York. Gaylin suggests we maintain a population of what he calls *neomorts*—persons whose brains no longer function, but whose bodies can still be kept alive when hooked up to machines. Gaylin says that "with the advent of new techniques in medicine, we are now capable of maintaining visceral (organ) functions without ... any [of the higher brain] functions that define a person." This would make it possible for surgeons to maintain colonies of "living dead bodies"—all of various tissue types—for use as organ donors.

Each year 365,000 people die as a result of damage to the brain. Many of them could be maintained as neomorts, where their bodies were kept alive artificially for surgeons to use as "organ farms." In this state all those characteristics that define an individual would not be present. There would be no intellectual faculties, no memory, no consciousness. They would be bodies but not people.

Maintaining a large population of neomorts would enable surgeons to have a supply of organs that would not have to be used at a moment's notice. Rather, they could be used when the conditions for the optimum success of the transplant were present. Neomorts also could be a source of regenerative tissues such as blood, skin, and bone marrow, and the tissues and fluids would always be fresh and free of any diseases.

According to Gaylin, "medical students could practice routine physical operations... standard and more difficult diagnostic procedures" on neomorts without fear of consequences. They could also study the progression of artificially induced diseases of the blood and organs. And a population of neomorts, maintained with their body parts catalogued for compatability, would end much waste of vitally needed organs.

The idea of neomorts means, of course, we have to revise the definition of death. No longer would death be signified by death of the heart. According to Stanford's Norman Shumway, the pioneering heart surgeon, "The brain in the 1970s and in the light of modern-day medical technology... is the criterion for death." Since many types of brain damage are completely irreversible, this suggests the death of the brain should represent the death of the individual. In May 1972 this criterion was legally established as a definition of death as a result of a suit against Dr. R. R. Lower of the Medical College of Virginia. Lower was charged with killing a heart donor by removing his heart to use for a transplant. He in turn contended that the patient had suffered irreversible brain damage and was therefore dead before the heart was removed. The jury ruled in favor of Lower, stating in their decision that brain damage was an adequate indicator of death.

A single jury decision in such matters is not definitive. The definition of death is still a hotly debated topic. In 1975, twenty-one-year-old Karen Ann Quinlan sustained massive brain damage as a result of ingesting large quantities of both alcohol and barbiturates. The doctors examining her stated that the damage that resulted to her brain tissue was irreversible and that there was no hope of her ever regaining consciousness. Yet when her parents petitioned the courts to allow their daughter to be taken off the machines that were sustaining her, the court refused to comply. They would not accept irreversible brain damage and loss of intellectual function as the definition of death. Later, however, the court reversed itself and allowed Quinlan to be taken off the life-assisting machines. As of this writing she has neither died nor regained consciousness.

No matter what the potential benefit to medical science, it is unlikely that neomorts will remain anything more than a concept for some time to come. The moral, legal, and even aesthetic reasons for using them are simply unacceptable in our society; the ends clearly do not justify the means. But as history shows, social values change— and the future may hold even more unthinkable realities.

REGENERATING OF WHOLE BODY PARTS

Some organisms have the ability to regrow entire parts of themselves. There are trees, for example, that can reproduce from a single branch. Salamanders can regrow missing limbs. Lizards can regrow their tails, which comprise about a fourth of their body weight. Starfish can lose up to half of their bodies and still regrow the missing parts.

Humans, however, have extremely limited ability to regenerate damaged tissue. We can regrow small portions of our livers, thyroid glands, bone, spleen, blood, and skin, but to do this, most of the original tissue must remain. With lower animals such as salamanders, a limb can regenerate even if the entire part is removed. If, like salamanders, lizards, and other reptiles, we were able to regrow missing body parts, there would obviously be no need for transplantation.

Rats have about the same low level of regenerative ability as humans. And in a startling experiment, Dr. Robert Becker, professor of orthopedics at New York's Upstate Medical Center, was able to cause rats to regrow small portions of amputated limbs. By implanting electrodes in the rats' stumps and keeping a steady flow of electricity into the tissues, Becker was able to get his rats to regenerate a substantial portion of a limb.

How did this come about? For years it has been known that there is a small electrical field surrounding the body of animals and humans which results from the constant electrical activity of nerves and muscles in transmitting impulses and in contracting. When, in the early 1960s, Becker began to study this electrical field surrounding salamanders, he observed that the field underwent specific changes when a limb was amputated and when the limb regenerated, and that the intensity and type of charge could be measured.

But when he began to investigate rats, he discovered that the changes in the field surrounding a rat after amputation were not the same as those in salamanders. Becker reasoned that the rats might not be able to regenerate simply because the necessary electrical changes didn't occur. And by implanting his electrodes to reproduce the kinds of changes in the field of a rat that occur in that of a salamander during regeneration of a limb, he was able to get the rats to regenerate.

Although so far there have been no experiments attempting to regenerate limbs in humans using electrodes, research suggests that electrical stimulation may help humans heal faster. Researchers at the Orthopedic Research Laboratories at Columbia University found that by placing electrodes over the site of a broken bone, low-frequency electrical pulsing could speed up repair. In some cases, bones were healed in just 50 percent of the time that it usually takes for healing to occur. At present, Becker is experimenting with electrodes as a means of aiding the body to repair damaged hearts.

In other promising research, Dr. Cynthia Illingworth of Children's Hospital in Sheffield, England, has shown that until a child is eleven or so a finger that is not damaged below the first joint will often regenerate spontaneously if it is left alone. Indeed, one patient, age five, was able to regrow the complete fingertip—including bone, nail, and skin—without medical intervention. This suggests that if the basis of these regenerative powers is chemical, and we lose these powers as we grow older, it may be possible for biochemists to find the right combination of chemicals which are produced by children but that are no longer present in an adult. Dr.

Dan Neufeld of George Washington University, who has been working on a project of trying to chemically induce limb regeneration, feels sure regeneration is possible. "Can man regenerate? I feel quite sure he can." And he adds, "I'd give up on this project if I didn't believe this."

Transplants have come a remarkably long way since they were first attempted in the late 1940s. Kidney and cornea transplants are routine procedures, and more people now survive the kidney transplant operation than die. Yet, many other types of transplants are still experimental. They represent one of medicine's frontiers. With each successful kidney transplant, researchers learn more about how the immune system operates, how the body learns to tolerate foreign proteins and also fights disease. And we are approaching a time when other transplant operations will also yield valuable results.

But because of the problems of rejection and organ supply, transplanted organs will not be of benefit to everyone. For them, however, there may be hope from another area of medicine—the new technology of bionics.

5. The New Technology of Bionics

Specialized organs and systems—sense, digestion, and reproduction—have evolved over several million years to enable ever more complex forms of life to function and survive. As a result, there are organs of amazing design sophistication and efficiency. A frog's eye is able to locate and identify any insect moving within its tongue range. Geese have such highly developed eye-brain coordination that they can navigate accurately over extremely long distances, apparently through a kind of visual alignment and recognition of stars and star positions, just like sailors with sextants and chronometers.

For centuries men have tried to copy nature's designs; Leonardo da Vinci's notebooks, for example, are filled with designs for flying machines modeled after birds. And in September 1960, at Wright-Patterson Air Force Base in Dayton, Ohio, under the sponsorship of the Air Force, scientists interested in utilizing nature's designs in producing instruments and machines came together to formally create a science for studying these processes and a technology for mimicking them. At this conference the word *bionics* was coined, from the Greek words *bios* (meaning life) and *ics* (meaning "having the nature of"). Air Force psychiatrist, mathematician, and electronics expert Jack Steele defined the word more precisely as "the science of systems which function after the manner of, or in a manner characteristic of or resembling, living systems."

At that time the Air Force was concerned with learning from living creatures ways to build better devices for defense. For example, early experimenters examined how snails were able to determine direction through sensing their position in reference to the earth's north-south magnetic field. Other researchers studied the skin texture of porpoises for possible use as coatings on ships to decrease water resistance and increase speed and fuel efficiency.

Of course, the study of bionics is concerned with more than simply Defense Department inquiries. It is also concerned with such large problems as the creation of artificial intelligence for use in computers and the creation of replacement body parts for use in medicine and life extension.

Bionics is a hybrid technology. Its researchers have degrees not only in biology, and zoology, but also in medicine, engineering, mathematics, and physics, and in chemistry, electronics, psychology, and logic. The field benefits from research in almost every other area, from textiles (for example, lightweight fabrics for parachutes modeled after birds' wings), to the microscopic etching of metals required to build the ultraminiaturized memory circuits needed to create artificial intelligence, and similar new areas. In medical bionics, many replacement parts have resulted from developments in seemingly unrelated fields.

The materials used in bionics are mostly names new to this century: miracle fibers such as Orlon, Dacron, nylon; plastics such as polyurethane, methylmethacrylate, and polyethylene; exotic metals such as titanium, chromium cobalt alloys, silicon compounds, various stainless steels, and ticonium alloys.

The principal benefit of these new materials is that they are not usually rejected by the body's immune system. Since the immune system recognizes only proteins, and since these new materials are not made of proteins, they may escape the immune system's attack. Not only are these materials compatable with our tissues, but many plastic and metal implants serve as scaffolds on which the body can grow new tissue. A swelling, damaged aorta, once a common and certain cause of death, can now be easily corrected by implanting a scaffold of Dacron, sewing it to the weakened artery, and then allowing nature to take its slightly altered course, covering the scaffold with healthy new tissue.

Replacement parts can take the place of a worn or defective limb or organ and often even duplicate much of the original part's function. There are kidneys that work, veins that carry blood, hearts that pump, all made of principally inorganic materials. Electronic heart pacemakers, synthetic muscles, and fingertip sensors are all being manufactured now, and new innovations in technology show promise that soon the deaf will hear, the blind will see, and the lame will walk.

There are four kinds of bionic equipment, some worn outside, some implanted inside: prosthetic, primarily external devices such as dentures and limbs; replacement, such as man-made shoulder joints; synthetic, such as tendons constructed of man-made fibers; and artificial, such as machines that take the place of organs.

PROSTHESIS: FROM LONG JOHN SILVER
TO THE SIX-MILLION-DOLLAR MAN

If most of us know anything about the history of prosthetic devices, it is probably through the character of that pirate of *Treasure Island,* Long John Silver, who, having lost his leg in a sword duel, replaced it with a peg leg that was secured in a special hole in the deck of his ship whenever he was at the wheel. Likewise, we may recall Captain Hook, the character in *Peter Pan* whose hand that was bitten off by a crocodile was replaced by a hook, a good weapon for a pirate but unquestionably not good for fine manipulations. And indeed peg legs and hooks were the major prosthetic surrogates of missing appendages for hundreds of years.

However a bionic device with probably a longer, if seemingly less dramatic, history is—false teeth. Dentures began in Egypt 3,000 years ago when the Pharoahs had their missing teeth replaced with carved bone and ivory attached with fine golden wire. Roman dentists were also adept at carving and fashioning false teeth from animal and human bones. If the teeth were carved well, they worked well, but it is very difficult to fit false teeth to the changing surfaces of someone's gums. In the fifteenth century, dentures were made from teeth carved from ivory, and fixed to a wooden plate that covered the gums—an apparatus so uncomfortable it was used mainly for cosmetic purposes and was removed during eating. Later, in the nineteenth century, denture makers, borrowing a technique from jewelry making called "swaging," were able to construct dentures suitable for use while eating. Using lead and zinc molds taken from plaster impressions of a person's mouth, the dentists pressed (swaged) gold into a replica of the mouth, glued hard rubber to it, and then attached porcelain teeth to the rubber. It was not until the 1930s that this process gave way to the acrylic plastics used to produce dentures today.

However, dentures, though important, are nowhere near as sophisticated as some of the new prosthetic devices now being produced.

Bionic Sight

Aside from glasses, which were invented by the Chinese in the tenth century, there have been no man-made devices available that could restore sight. Now, however, bionics has made possible the restoration of sight in many otherwise hopeless situations.

Corneal scarring occurs in the eye as a result of injury, and also from little understood changes in eye chemistry. The result of these changes is that the clear outermost eye tissue, the cornea, through which light must pass in order to enter the eye, becomes opaque and gradually causes blindness. This disease, which primarily affects older adults, has no known cure other than the transplantation of donated corneal tissue from the eye of a cadaver.

Usually partial corneal grafts, in which surgeons replace only some of the layers of clear tissue, are sufficient, but sometimes the scarring is so extensive that the entire cornea must be replaced. However, only one out of four full corneal grafts is successful, because the fluid behind the cornea exerts an outward pressure, making it difficult to hold the graft in place for the month or so that it takes to join it to the eye. Sneezing or coughing also can dislodge the transplanted cornea.

Because of these problems, William Stone, Jr., an opthalmologist-surgeon at the Massachusetts Eye and Ear Infirmary in Boston, designed a bionic replacement for damaged corneas made of clear acrylic plastic similar to that used in making both dentures and jet fighter windshields. The plastic cornea screws into a socket that resembles a tiny collar button, and the socket is sutured in place on the surface of the eye just in front of the iris. This screw-in cornea, which can be removed or exchanged to suit optical prescriptions, has so far been implanted in 400 people.

Medical technology has also come up with a bionic lens. The lens of the eye, located just behind the colored iris, is subject to clouding as a result of cataracts. This causes the lens to darken and scatter or block incoming light. Usually, when cataracts occur, the only treatment is surgical. The surgeon makes a small incision in the white of the eye and inserts a tiny suction device that pulls out the entire lens. The incision is then closed and light can again freely pass into the eye.

Unfortunately, after the lens is removed there is no way for the eye to focus incoming light without the aid of thick glasses or contact lenses. Use of glasses is often not convenient because one must change glasses whenever he wishes to look from a near object into the distance, which makes tasks like driving very difficult. Contact lenses, set for medium vision, combined with a pair of bifocal glasses, can solve the problem, but contact lenses cannot be comfortably worn by everyone.

Dr. Norman Jaffe, of the University of Miami, solved the problem by devising an artificial implantable lens. Using polymethacrylate—a close relative of the acrylic plastics used for artificial corneas—he had the tiny bionic lens ground for a specific, fixed prescription, and set it in a soft ring of Dacron fiber. Using the Dacron as an anchor, Jaffe sutured the lens in place behind the iris. The plastic lens cannot change focus, but when used with glasses, near perfect vision often results. This artificial lens is presently being used by at least a hundred opthalmic surgeons around the country to replace cataract-scarred natural lenses.

But not all cases of blindness result from a degeneration of the cornea or lens. Many of the approximately 110,000 people in the United States totally without sight have lost their vision as a result of more profound damage to the eyes. One presently untreatable form of blindness results from glaucoma, in which the liquid behind the lens called the aqueous humor overproduces and builds up pressure to the point where it destroys the delicate light-sensing surface of the retina. Blindness from nerve-degeneration diseases and birth defects which damage the retina or its nerve connections to the brain is also currently untreatable. However, even here there is hope and its source is television technology.

The television camera works much like the eye in that it converts light into electrical impulses after the light has been focused by a lens. The kind and quality of the electrical impulses sent out by a TV camera are much different from the electrical currents sent from the eye to the brain; however, it is theoretically possible to make use of the electrical impulses emitted by a TV camera to produce the sensations of sight in the brain.

Opthalmologist William H. Dobelle, director of a neuro-prosthesis program at the Institute for Biomedical Engineering at the University of Utah, studied the kind of impulses a normal eye sends to the brain when it is stimulated by light and then created a special computer designed to convert the electrical impulses from a TV camera into impulses similar to those emitted by the retina. Dobelle then designed a square of Teflon and platinum, and this was implanted into the skulls of two blind volunteers near the parts of their brains responsible for decoding information sent by the eyes and converting that information into sight. The small electrical grids in the two volunteers' heads were then connected to TV cameras and focused on some very simple shapes. Both patients, as soon as electrical stimulation started reaching their brains, reported "seeing" flashes of light—called phosphenes. Dobelle reported that one patient who had been blind for twenty-eight years said he "saw" colorless, flickering phosphenes about the size of a coin at arm's length.

Since then Dobelle has gone one step further and devised an artificial-sight system whereby a thirty-three-year-old man, who has been blind for ten years, is able to plug into a computer that enables him to "see" electronic signals in his brain. Sixty-four electrodes were implanted in the visual cortex of the man's brain, tiny wires were attached to each electrode and run through an opening in his skull, and the wires were attached to a graphite plug sewn into his skin. When the plug is inserted in a computer attached to a TV camera, the man can read Braille letters in the form of dots of light and distinguish horizontal and vertical lines. Dobelle feels that the experiment indicates that long-term implants are possible, and foresees the day whan a TV camera can be placed in a blind person's eye socket and connected through a miniature computer to electrodes in the brain. Although much more experiment will be required to make the transition between simple patterns and more sophisticated black and white pictures, Dr. Willem Kolff, a pioneer in bionic research, believes that eventually this kind of artificial sight will give blind people vision that will appear similar to "pictures on the scoreboard of the Houston Astrodome."

The development of any artificial organ, Dobelle points out, happens gradually. "First there is speculation, then there is hope, and then there is promise. Sensory prostheses have clearly gone from the point of speculation to the point where there is real hope." And promise appears imminent.

Bionic Hearing

Once the only device to augment hearing was an ear trumpet. This funnel-like device was of some benefit to those whose hearing loss resulted from overgrowth, or ossification, of the three sound-transmitting bones in the middle ear (the hammer, anvil, and stirrup), which increased the rigidity of these bones, hampering their ability to transmit sound vibrations to the inner ear and brain. This type of hearing loss is mechanical rather than the result of nerve damage or inner ear damage, and so sound-amplifying devices can increase the amount of sound vibration and somewhat offset the hearing loss caused by the ossified middle ear bones. But the sound-magnifying ability of the ear trumpet is extremely limited, and better amplification techniques were needed.

With the invention of the telegraph in 1837 by Samuel F. B. Morse, and its subsequent refinement into an expanded commercial communications network, the use of electricity became both practical and dependable. Sensing the great possibilities inherent in the transmission of messages electrically, Alexander Graham Bell set out to discover a way to convert sound vibrations into electrical impulses and then back into sound. His goal was *not* to invent the telephone but to create a machine for aiding those with hearing loss. Finally, in 1876, Bell succeeded in converting sound to electrical impulses and back again, with the result being the invention of the telephone instead of the hearing aid. But for all its utility, Bell's invention was unable to amplify sound. With the invention of the electrical transformer in 1885, however, effective amplification of sound was possible, and in 1902 a man named Miller Reese Hutchinson created the first electrical hearing aid. Later, transistors and miniaturized circuitry helped to make that instrument a much more compact apparatus that could be worn entirely in or behind the ear.

While many cases of simple hearing loss can be corrected with the use of hearing aids, the more profound types of deafness, affecting an estimated 300,000 Americans, must be approached quite differently. In many cases, the answer is the surgical implantation of a bionic replacement for the damaged ear bones. In this operation, developed in 1952 by Dr. Samuel Rosen of New York's Mount Sinai Hospital, what looks like a short, round-headed nail made of Teflon is inserted into the middle ear through a tiny incision in the ear drum, and the defective earbones are removed. One end of the implant rests on the "window" of the cochlea, the snail-shaped inner ear; the other end touches the ear drum. When sound vibrations strike the ear drum, they are converted into mechanical vibrations that travel along the new implant and then stimulate the inner ear window. Inside the cochlea, fluids allow the vibrations to travel further, where they stimulate the tiny nerve endings that convert the mechanical sound vibrations into the electrical impulses that are then sent to the brain. With Rosen's implant the hearing process can be restored to near normal levels in many cases. In the U.S. alone, approximately 5,000 of these ear implantations are performed every year.

In many cases, deafness results from an inability of the nerve to receive sound vibrations from the inner ear and convert them into electrical impulses. Here the Teflon implant has no practical value and other methods of restoring hearing must be attempted. Researchers working under Dr. William House at the Ear Research Institute in Los Angeles are experimenting with a bionic implant device that electronically converts sound into electrical impulses for the direct stimulation of the part of the brain responsible for hearing.

The "ear" consists of a miniaturized microphone and amplifying circuit that changes sound into a tiny trickle of electrical current. This electronic device is surgically implanted into the ear, taking the place of both the ear drum and the middle ear bones. Auditory nerves carry information to the brain through a complex process that uses chemical energy to produce an electrical impulse. The bionic implant, acting as an artificial ear drum, middle ear, and nerve, rests near the damaged nerve inside the inner ear and electrically stimulates it into carrying sound information to the brain. In preliminary tests, House's bionic ear enabled some profoundly deaf people to recognize sounds such as telephones and doorbells ringing. So far conventional speech discrimination is poor, but changes in the system are expected to improve results.

All the limitations of conventional hearing aids—low fidelity, feedback, the need for a tight-fitting ear mold, and the presence of an externally visible device—would be corrected by a completely implantable device. Except for the lack of a small, rechargeable battery for a power source, such a "hearing aid within the head" is possible now. Present batteries of the appropriate size just are not durable enough to supply power for more than a few weeks, and it obviously is impractical to replace a battery surgically every two weeks.

However, recently a battery was developed for heart pacemakers that could be recharged inside the person. While this battery is still too big at present for ear implantation, Dr. Richard Goode of Stanford Medical Center, developer of a hearing aid implantable inside the head, expects that a rechargeable battery about the size of a quarter or smaller will be available. In 1976, Dr. Goode estimated that a patient-ready model of the implantable hearing device would appear on the market within five years.

Bionic Limbs

Over the last twenty-five years, the peg leg of Long John Silver has been transformed into something much closer to the bionic limbs of Steve Austin, hero of *Six Million Dollar Man*. Much of the development of bionic arms has come out of research first begun by the Atomic Energy Commission in the early 1950s.

With the advent of nuclear power, ways had to be devised that would enable a technician, working at a distance from his materials, to handle radioactive substances with great precision and power. The task of mixing plutonium into pellets of exact weight, for example, had to be performed with delicate exactitude, but the task of lifting lead-shielded containers required tremendous strength. The first bionic device to cope with these problems looked like a metal glove that fit onto the hand of a technician sitting in a shielded room watching his work through a window several feet thick. Through an elaborate electronic setup, the electric glove was wired into huge hydraulic clamps in the inside room. Sensors in the glove measured each movement of the technician's hand and sent electrical impulses to the hydraulic pumps in the other room, which then moved the clamps.

The clamps could rotate, grip, pour, and mimic nearly every movement of a human hand. It was important that the clamps be able to accurately sense pressure or else a simple move of the technician's hand might crush an important nuclear component. For this purpose, certain crystals called piezoelectric crystals—long used in record player pick-up arms to convert the needle vibrations into electric current—were modified into pressure-sensitive sensors to handle delicate tasks.

At the same time, research in England was being done on myoelectricity (*myos* is Greek for muscle), which is concerned with the electric current that occurs on the surface of a muscle when it is ordered by a nerve to move. This led to the development of myoelectric sensors capable of accurately sensing the electricity surging over a muscle during a contraction and amplifying that into sufficient current to drive a bionic limb.

With piezoelectric sensors capable of measuring pressure and myoelectric sensors capable of sensing muscle contraction—plus the kinds of electronic circuits used by the AEC to convert hand movements into clamp movement—it became possible to build a bionic arm capable of sensing the pressure on its "fingers" and able to respond accurately to the wearer through the electricity in the muscles of his stump. It would have been possible to build such an arm, except that in the 1950s the electronic circuitry of the AEC's clamp filled several rooms, and the power came from huge hydraulic pumps that weighed several tons.

In 1952 eight-year-old Karen McKibben was stricken with a case of polio so severe that she became paralyzed in both arms and legs. Her father, Dr. Joseph McKibben, a nuclear physicist working for the government in Los Angeles, then began applying some of the techniques used by the AEC to try to enable his daughter to move her hands. Working with Dr. Vernon L. Nickel, an orthopedic surgeon at Rancho Los Amigos Rehabilitation Hospital, a Los Angeles center doing extensive work on artificial limbs, McKibben succeeded in devising a gas-powered bionic muscle. It consisted of a fishing line woven into a tube, much like a Chinese finger puzzle, which enabled the tube to relax and contract, just as a real muscle does. Inside the tube McKibben put a narrow, airtight balloon. When the balloon was filled with carbon dioxide gas, the tube became thicker and shorter, like a muscle contraction.

This device, extremely simple to make, became the primary source of power for bionic limbs in the 1950s. Balloons, inside wire mesh nets, were filled with CO_2 gas kept in a small cylinder. When the muscle needed to be tightened, the CO_2 rushed into the balloon; when it needed to be loosened, a valve opened and the gas escaped. Unfortunately, this type of apparatus was bulky, noisy, and suitable only for those who had lost the use of their limbs, not those whose limbs had been amputated.

Even greater advances have occurred since then. The space program techniques of electronic miniaturization have reached such an advanced state that all of the room-filling electronic circuitry used in the early AEC clamps can now easily be fitted inside a light plastic bionic arm. Tiny electric motors are also available, capable of exerting a remarkable amount of force and requiring only very small amounts of electricity. These plus the myoelectric and piezoelectric sensors have enabled researchers to build a fully bionic arm.

Reid Hilton was a twenty-four-year-old karate expert from Santa Ana, California, when he lost his right arm just below the elbow in an auto accident. Fortunately, at the time of the accident a research team at Rancho Los Amigos Hospital, headed by Dr. Vert

Mooney, had just finished creating a prototype bionic arm weighing only 8 pounds and powered by a rechargeable electric powerpack and tiny motors, all inside the arm. Hilton's arm, installed in 1975, has a grip strength of 40 pounds—versus only 25 pounds for the average man. Electrically connected to the muscles inside his upper arm, it responds almost like a real arm, doing nearly anything he wants it to do—including such fine movements as picking small objects off the floor and tying shoelaces and, of course, the larger movements required in karate. Inside the fingertips are sensors that pulse, sending messages back to him, and preventing him from exerting too much pressure on any object. In 1976, Mooney estimated the arm would be available on a production basis in about five years to those who needed it.

REPLACEMENT AND SYNTHETIC PARTS: BETTER THAN NATURE

The innovations in bionic prosthetic devices are spectacular, but for sheer *numbers* they don't compare to the hardware catalog of things that may be used to repair defective parts inside the human body. From great toe joint to skull plate, here is a spare-parts list of things available to replace defective bones, joints, muscles, and the like. In some cases, they are superior in function to nature's original.

Bionic Joints and Bones

In arthroplasty—plastic surgery of joints—there have been a great many successes with bionic substitutes. Injuries to bones and joints are common, the result of fractures, arthritis, bursitis, and various degenerative diseases.

The first experiments with bionic joints, in the early 1950s, consisted of cutting and shaping the ball on the top of the femur, the long bone inside the thigh, which fits into the socket of the hip joint, and then fitting an artificial stainless steel ball onto the end of the carved bone. Because it was difficult to get a perfect match between the size of the stainless steel ball and the hip socket into which it fit, this method was not always successful. In cases where the socket had also deteriorated, this early operation was of no use. And often, as a result of wear, the steel ball became detached from the bone.

But in 1954, Dr. John Charnley of Wrightington Hospital in Wigan, England, hit upon the idea of creating a total hip joint out of Teflon and steel that would enable a surgeon to replace the entire ball and socket assembly. Charnley hoped that his bionic hip would help not only those suffering from a degeneration of the ball of the femur, but also those suffering from a degeneration of the socket. With a total hip replacement there would no longer be problems of exact fit; his bionic joint would be designed to take the place of both elements of the hip joint, and could therefore be fitted perfectly outside the body before implantation.

Charnley's hip-joint design closely resembled nature's original design, except that the ball, made of stainless steel, and the socket, made of Teflon, were made smaller in order to decrease friction. The hip joint was cemented in place with acrylic plastic glue. Charnley believed the artificial ball-and-socket hip should be made to last at least ten years, since those usually in need of bionic hips are around age sixty and require a prosthesis that will last at least as long as their probable remaining years without further operations. But simulated wear conditions showed the Teflon would not last longer than two or three years.

Then in 1962, one of Charnley's technicians made the accidental discovery that plastic polyethylene, which is used to make everything from model toys to car interiors, would wear less in three weeks than Teflon would in one day. That year Charnley began replacing degenerated hip joints with those consisting of stainless steel balls fitted into polyethylene sockets. Since then he has performed over 5,000 hip replacement operations, and has refined his procedure to such an extent that he is now able to perform as many as six total hip replacements in one day, with each separate operation requiring only about an hour.

Bionic parts have also been developed for other joints. For joints of the hand, finger, and great toe, the principal material used is Silastic, a silicone plastic. For artificial wrists, knees, elbows, shoulders, and ankles, a variety of materials are used: Silastic, stainless steel, cobalt, chromium, polyethylene, and other alloys and plastics.

Because of their multiple capabilities, joints are frequently difficult to reproduce. The ankle, for instance, consists of six main bones that are designed to bend and flex in several directions at once, allowing us to walk and run on level surfaces and climb mountain trails. In addition, the ankle is also designed to compensate for the placement of the foot. Climbing a ladder puts different stresses on the ankle than does dancing or walking in sand.

When Dr. Theodore Waugh, an orthopedic surgeon at the University of California at Irvine, set out to make an artificial ankle, he tried to mimic nature's own design. Using a chromium cobalt alloy, Waugh made a T-shaped pin that could be cemented inside the tibia, the largest of the two bones in the calf. Then, on top of the talus, the main bone in the ankle, he cemented a dome-shaped chromium cobalt base plate. The head of the "T" then rested upside down on the dome and was free to bend and move in the same way as the original ankle bones. Natural fluids from the body kept the joint lubricated.

The ankle weighs only 5 ounces but is stronger than natural ankle bones. In the fifteen operations that Waugh has performed so far, most patients have been up and walking with crutches within five days, and have walked unaided within a month. One of the good things about the operation, according to Waugh, is that any competent orthopedic surgeon can do it, and thus it has the potential to bring relief to thousands of crippled persons.

In addition to developing bionic replacements of nearly every human joint, researchers are also working on making artificial bones. Early implants made of the strong, light metal titanium may soon give way to glass and other forms of bone substitute. Dr. Larry Hench, director of the University of Florida's Biomedical Engineering Program, calls his new glass bones "bioglass." This material begins with glass very similar to ordinary window glass, made of pure quartz sand. To this is added sodium oxide, calcium, and phosphorous, which have the effect of tricking the body into thinking the bioglass is real bone. As these chemicals are slowly released, like tiny time pills, the natural bone that it joins slowly fuses with the bioglass. The new substance promises to be far superior to titanium because it will form a "scaffold" on which normal bone can grow. The scaffold, which is like a skeleton within a skeleton, will then become incorporated inside the newly grown bone and the result will be a hip, arm, thigh, or even teeth far superior in strength to the original.

Bionic Tendons, Ligaments, and Muscles

Ligaments lash bone to bone, and tendons—long ropes of tough protein fibers—lash muscle to bone. Both have poor regenerative ability and cannot always heal if they break or are stressed excessively. When a tendon breaks, it may be pulled by the attached contracting muscles, so that it becomes "lost" in the arm or leg and must be located surgically.

In the past, broken tendons were repaired with surgery, and the results were extremely unpredictable. Later, techniques were evolved that removed a ligament from a joint and joined that ligament to the muscle and bone, using it to take the place of the tendon. These ligament-for-tendon operations were generally successful, but they had the drawback of weakening the joint from which the ligament was removed.

Dr. William E. Harrison, Jr., of Maimonidies Hospital in New York has been able to make "scaffolds" using Dacron, an inert synthetic, which is woven into a tube design, slipped over the broken ends of the ligament or tendon, and sewn into place. With the limb immobilized, the Dacron scaffold allows a new segment of ligament or tendon to grow. Using this technique Harrison reports great success in several experiments. In fact, the bionically reinforced ligament or tendon is even stronger than the original because it incorporates the Dacron into its repaired structure.

There have also been experiments on artificial skeletal muscles, which help us to maintain our upright posture. J. D. Helmer, a bio-engineer at Batelle Columbus Laboratories in Ohio, has devised a synthetic muscle made from silicone rubber—an inert, long-lasting type of rubber—and Dacron. The design is similar to the "muscle" in the early gas-powered bionic arm: a Dacron sheath, woven like a Chinese finger puzzle, is fitted over a rubber tube and joined to the tendon. When tension from the tendon pulls the sheath tight, it causes it to squeeze the rubber tube; when the sheath is pulled, the elastic rubber exerts a back pressure and the effect is that of a muscle—opposing the tension with an equal and opposite tension. Helmer and his associates have implanted the muscles in sheep so that they have been able to walk with nearly normal gait four weeks after the operation.

Bionic Circulation: Heart Valves and Blood

Breakdowns in the circulatory system, which includes the heart and miles of arteries, veins, and capillaries, are still responsible for more deaths in the U.S. than any other single cause. Heart attacks, hardening of the arteries, strokes, blood clots clogging the vessels, high blood pressure—as well as other circulatory illnesses resulting from injury, stress, or disease—shorten our potential life spans by almost twenty years. In this area there has been extremely intense research and some encouraging accomplishments.

At a time when most Americans began wearing Orlon on the outside, in the form of sweaters, one man started wearing his Orlon on the inside—in the form of rebuilt arteries. That was in 1953, when Dr. Charles Hugnagel of Georgetown University, operating on a wounded Korean war G.I., repaired a bullet-damaged femoral artery, the major artery carrying oxygenated blood to the leg, by fitting an Orlon graft or scaffold into the blood vessel. Later, Hufnagel also fitted an Orlon graft into the patient's weakened aorta. Both these blood vessels are subject to constant flexing, squeezing, and pressure, and until Orlon became available there was almost no way these major arteries could be repaired.

But the Orlon Hufnagel used had the disadvantage of being extremely easy to collapse. An implant of soft woven Orlon carrying blood to the lungs, for example, could kink like a twisted garden hose, and the result would be a quick and painful death. In 1955, however, Dr. Sterling Edwards, of the Medical College of Alabama, came upon the idea of crimping the synthetic arteries so they resembled the pleated flexible section of a flex-straw. These crimped arteries, now made of Dacron and Teflon, were both flexible and resistant to kinking. In addition, the use of these synthetic materials made the artificial arteries 100 percent inert, so that there was no problem of an immune reaction.

The implantation of crimped synthetic arteries of Dacron or Teflon is now the preferred treatment for such diseases as aortic aneurisms, the irregular ballooning-out of the aorta, the main blood vessel in the body, as a result of a weak muscle wall. Aortic aneurisms can be corrected with the use of bionic arteries, and the chances of patient survival are very good. Famed heart specialist Dr. Michael E. De Bakey of Baylor Medical College in Houston, who has personally performed more than 2,000 of these aortic implants, claims that nearly 80 percent of his patients undergoing surgery for aortic aneurism survive at least five years without problems.

Other arteries, damaged as a result of aneurisms or clogged as a result of hardening of the arteries, can also be replaced with artificial Dacron or Teflon arteries. De Bakey, for example, has now implanted more than 5,200 bionic arterial grafts. The success rate for replacement of a femoral artery, for instance, is even higher than that of the aortic replacement operation. Surgeons now have at their disposal a bionic replacement for nearly every artery and vein.

Heart valves have also benefitted from the availability of new materials. These valves open and close 100,000 times a day, and with the constant flexing it is a wonder they last as long as they do. However, because of rheumatic fever or degeneration brought on by age, the valves may no longer be able to form a tight enough seal inside the heart and the result is that the heart pumps progressively less oxygenated blood, causing the whole body's functioning to deteriorate.

Twenty years ago corrective surgery on the heart was considered an impossibility. In 1883 the famous American surgeon C.A.T. Billroth was quoted as saying "Let no man who hopes to retain the respect of his medical brethren dare to operate on the human heart." Since then, thousands of heart valve operations have been performed. Drs. Denton Cooley and Michael De Bakey of Baylor University, for example, have between them implanted an estimated 7,500 bionic valves.

The first artificial heart valve, developed by Dr. Albert Starr, a heart surgeon at the University of Oregon Medical School in Portland, and M. Lowell Edwards, an aerospace engineer, was composed

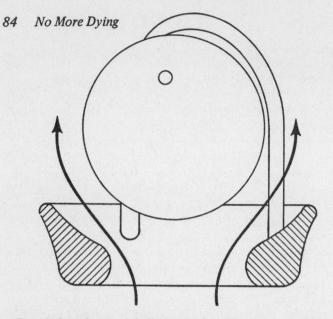

Starr-Edwards caged ball heart valve. The arrows indicate the direction of blood flow. Blood which tried to flow in the other direction would shut off the valve.

of three parts: a housing, lip, and ball. The housing was a small basket-shaped cage made of titanium. The cage was open at one end and rounded at the other, having the general shape of the crown of a ten-gallon hat, and was composed of three strands of titanium wire. Inside the hatlike housing was a small ball made of Teflon. The opening of the cage was formed in such a way that the ball could move freely but not come out of the cage. Instead, the Dacron-covered lip of the titanium cage and the ball, when touching each other, formed a perfect seal, cutting off the flow of blood just like a natural valve.

On March 10, 1960, a team of Harvard University Medical School surgeons performed the first surgical valve replacement using the Starr-Edwards valve. They removed the patient's diseased valve and replaced it with the new invention, anchoring it to the heart with Dacron sutures. The bionic valve operated just like a natural valve. When the heart was filled with blood, the ball would seal the lip of the cage. When the heart contracted, back pressure forced the ball against the rounded end of the cage, allowing the blood to flow out.

Since the early days of heart valve replacement, the operation has become more or less commonplace. And another type of valve has been developed, by Hufnagel of Georgetown, that substitutes a plastic disk for the Starr-Edwards ball-and-cage type of valve.

One of the most far-reaching and exciting bionic possibilities affecting the circulatory system, as well as the rest of the body, is synthetic blood, a substance that is urgently needed, since today natural blood is not always available when required. In cases of severe injury, very often large quantities of blood are needed for transfusions. With rare types of blood, adequate quantities can be difficult to obtain and often there is the chance of transferring a donor's unknown disease to the injured person. Whole blood also has a shelf life of only about three weeks, and it is not uncommon for hospitals to have to throw away blood that is too old.

In 1966, Dr. Leland C. Clark, Jr., of the University of Cincinnati's College of Medicine, reported he had developed a synthetic blood based on fluorocarbon emulsions, the same chemicals used as propellants in aerosol spray cans. Fluorocarbons are chemically inert; under most circumstances they will not combine with any other chemicals, and since they are also not made of proteins they are not able to trigger an attack from the immune system. In addition, fluorocarbons can serve as a medium into which other chemicals can dissolve without their being affected in any way. In a series of experiments on dogs, cats, and mice, where the animal's natural blood was replaced with fluorocarbons, Clark noted that bionic blood was superior to real blood in its ability to hold oxygen molecules, and to make the bionic blood more like real blood such substances as platelets, clotting factors, and special proteins could be taken from real blood or manufactured synthetically.

For patients suffering from such diseases as aplastic anemia and leukemia, which require massive and frequent blood transfusions, fluorocarbon blood may prove to be an inexpensive substitute. And as Clark states, "there is no worry about hepatitis or other infections, because fluorocarbon blood would be sterile and would also produce no allergic reactions." In addition, Clark says, "it can be stored indefinitely, at least compared with real blood, which gradually loses its ability to store oxygen."

Bionic Erections

Biomedical engineers have applied their skill in areas other than those that relate directly to life extension. The problem of impotence, for example, though mainly psychosomatic, can result from physical dysfunction or injury.

Normal erections are reached when the corpus cavernosum—cavities inside the shaft of the penis—fill with blood. An intricate system of valves inside the corpus cavernosum allows blood to enter the organ but does not allow it to leave at as fast a rate. The result is that the penis grows larger from the buildup of blood pressure that occurs inside the cylindrical cavities. After the erection is reached the valves regulate the incoming and outgoing blood so that a firm erection is maintained. Damage to the valves, the corpus cavernosum, or a diminishing of the blood supply to the area can result in a man's inability to achieve the erection.

Urologist Brantley Scott, of Baylor Medical College in Houston, teamed up with neurologist William Bradley and biomedical engineer Gerald Timm, of University of Minnesota Hospital, to solve the medical problem by creating the first fully implantable bionic erection-assist device. This device, so far implanted in forty-six men, has proved to be completely successful. As Bradley explained, "it isn't *like* a real erection—it *is* a real erection—enlargement, growth in diameter . . . it's great."

The device is made of silicone rubber and consists of two collapsible cylinders that are surgically placed inside the corpus cavernosum in the shaft of the penis. Attached to the two cylinders is a tiny hose that connects to a small ball-shaped pump that is placed inside the scrotal sac. Next to the ball-shaped pump is a small, round reservoir that contains a sterile fluid. An erection is achieved by squeezing the pump, which in turn forces fluid from the reservoir into the two cylinders inside the penis. The bionic erection is kept firm by the pressure pumped into the cylinders. A valve keeps the fluid inside and maintains a full erection until the pressure is released by gently pressing the pump again. This device can maintain an erection for an indefinite amount of time, but it also allows full sensitivity and normal ejaculation.

It is also possible that, with the help of bionics, doctors will be able to reverse vasectomies. Dr. Erich E. Brueschke and others of the Illinois Institute of Technology Research in Chicago were able to use silicone-rubber tubing to connect the two ends of the severed vas deferens and restore fertility to vasectomized dogs. Twenty-six months after the operation, the dogs were able to ejaculate normal sperm without leakage.

There are several other kinds of replacement and synthetic equipment, and the list grows yearly. An artificial trachea made of Silastic has been implanted in several patients. Intervertebral disks made of Dacron and silicone have been implanted in chimpanzees. Artificial skin has been applied successfully on guinea pigs. There are skull plates, artificial jaws, Eustachian tube substitutes, plastic and latex rubber larynxes, and even a silicon rubber urinary sphincter. But perhaps the most fascinating category of bionics is that of artificial devices—machines that can take the place of organs.

ARTIFICIAL ORGANS: MAN OUT OF A MACHINE

In our time, machines no longer whine and clank—they hum or make no noise at all. Among these are the bionic devices for replacing kidneys, pancreas, liver, and heart.

Bionic Kidneys

The body's blood supply requires constant filtering if it is to sustain life, and kidney breakdown is among the biggest killers.

The toxins and wastes that build up in the body as a result of the metabolism's constant conversion of food products into energy would poison us within a few days if it were not for the filters of the kidneys. The kidneys are designed to remove these waste products and toxins from the system by first causing blood to pass through many miles of capillaries, which in turn force the blood through membranes that separate the smaller waste products from blood proteins and other vital molecules.

Willem Kolff, a young physician in Holland during World War II, began a research program designed to build an artificial kidney to take the place of diseased kidneys. Working at night to avoid discovery by the occupying Germans (since one reason for his research was to treat injured Dutch partisans), Kolff began experimenting with various ways of constructing synthetic kidneys. Using only the equipment the Nazis thought a physician should have, Kolff created a drumlike apparatus for circulating the blood over a large surface area of artificial membrane. Not having the benefits of today's highly advanced plastics and filters for creating plastic membranes, Kolff used cellophane sausage casings to act as filters. Although his machine (which looked like a miniature washing machine with rotating drums resting in a sugar water solution to "leach out" toxins) was primitive, it was successful. Ironically, Kolff's first patient was a woman later suspected of being a Nazi collaborator.

Kolff's cumbersome dialysis machine (dialysis is Greek for "dissolve") has since become no larger than a medium-sized television set. Kolff's "sugar water" solution, which draws toxins from the blood, has been refined to a liquid with a content similar to blood. Portable bionic kidneys are now available for home use. It is estimated that, world-wide, as many as 100,000 people have used kidney machines.

Now at the Institute of Biomedical Engineering at the University of Utah, Kolff believes that through miniaturization an electrodialysis unit can be implanted in the human body. In fact, he has already created a 5-pound artificial kidney, made to be worn like a backpack, that can filter out a person's blood toxins and wastes with as little as two hours of use per day.

Bionic Pancreas

Insulin regulates energy reactions inside the cells. Among other things, the pancreas supplies insulin to the body and thus enables it to store sugar as fat for later conversion to energy. Then this mechanism breaks down, the metabolism may go out of control.

Cells release sugar into the blood, break down their proteins into toxic wastes, and poison the body with excess toxins. When there is insufficient insulin in the body, the buildup of toxins in the blood begins to destroy the cells inside the eyes, brain, and blood vessels. Lack of insulin causes an imbalance of body salts and water which can lead to excessively low blood pressure, interrupting blood flow to the organs and brain damage.

Diabetes, the result of too little insulin in the blood, is one of the ten leading causes of death in the United States. Without treatment, a diabetic can expect to live only about twenty years. With daily insulin injections, or oral insulin, he can live fifty years. But insulin therapy cannot vary the amount of insulin in the blood to accurately meet the body's minute-to-minute needs. There is often too much or too little insulin. Thus, the metabolism of a diabetic, even with insulin therapy, is always upset, and his body is therefore always subject to damage.

Several groups of researchers are working on developing a bionic pancreas which would provide insulin to the body only when it is needed and in the correct amount. William L. Chick, of the Joslin Diabetes Foundation of Boston, is working on a preliminary model of an implantable pancreas that uses tissue from a normal pancreas, either human or animal. He places the tissue inside artificial capillaries and circulates blood over them. The capillaries are designed so that only insulin and other small molecules can pass through them, but not proteins or cells. Since this effectively isolates the pancreas tissue from the person's blood supply, there is no danger of a reaction by the immune system, and thus pancreas tissue from rats or other animals can be used as an insulin source. Insulin from man and many animals, including the cows which are the source of much of the insulin used in diabetic therapy, is similar and works the same in both the animals and man. Before the device can be tested in humans, however, a material must be found for making artificial capillaries that will not damage the patient's blood.

Chick's pancreas is not wholly artificial since it uses tissue from a natural pancreas, using a machine to measure the body's need for insulin and injecting the correct amount from a reservoir. The first such device was produced in 1962 by Arnold Kadish of the Metabolic Dynamics Foundation in Los Angeles. He adapted a machine originally designed to measure sugar levels in blood samples to a device which could make those measurements and inject insulin or sugar as needed by the body. This device, though large and slow, showed that a totally artificial pancreas was possible.

One of the most recent of the improved type of bionic pancreases was designed by J. Stuart Soeldner of Joslin and Kuo Wei Chang and Sol Aisenberg of the Whittaker Corporation Space Sciences Division. It consists of a glucose sensor disk implanted in the body and connected to a metering device which tells the patient how much sugar is in the blood and thereby the amount of insulin. (There is an inverse relationship between the level of sugar and the level of insulin in the blood.) The glucose sensor, which is about the size of a quarter, has already been tested in many rabbits and monkeys for as long as 117 days and has proved capable of accurately measuring changes in blood sugar.

Another sensor, about the size of a nickel, has been developed by Samuel P. Bessman of the University of Southern California School of Medicine, and is already being tested in humans. When the sensors are combined with insulin-regulating micro-pumps designed by Bessman, a complete artificial pancreas will be available. Bessman feels that there are no further technical impediments to the production of an artificial pancreas and that it is simply a matter of doing the necessary testing in animals before it is used by humans.

Bionic Liver

More than twenty-five English patients with acute liver failure have been successfully tested with a hemodialysislike device developed by Dr. Richard A. Willson of the University of Washington School of Medicine. Willson believes the unit can be miniaturized for portability. Other scientists are working on implantable livers.

Bionic Lungs

The lung is composed of membranes so that the maximum amount of surface area for gas exchange is available. As the blood passes over the membranes, it loses carbon dioxide and other gaseous metabolic wastes, and at the same time takes in oxygen. In 1953, Dr.

John H. Gibbon of the Jefferson Medical College in Virginia designed a heart-lung machine that could pump blood through the body and oxygenate it at the same time, thus enabling surgeons to bypass the blood vessel connections between heart and lungs during heart operations. With this machine, the era of open heart surgery began. Before that time the only way doctors could operate on the heart was to cool the patient's blood by circulating it through refrigeration coils to a low enough temperature (about 75 degrees) so that interrupting the blood flow for a short time would not cause any damage. But this only gave them about half an hour in which to work, precluding major surgery and always risking brain damage from the cooling or lack of oxygen.

But there have also been developments on bionic lungs per se. With further experimentation, a "paracorporeal membrane oxygenator," devised by Dr. E. Converse Peirce II of Bronx Veterans Administration Hospital in New York and tested successfully on dogs, could be made light enough, perhaps 10 to 15 pounds, so that it could be worn as a backpack. In addition, a lung built out of Silastic tubing encased in a flexible plastic envelope has been developed, by Dr. Louis R. Head and others at Chicago's Northwestern Memorial Hospital, and implanted in dogs and sheep.

A major test of artificial lungs, started in April 1975 and projected to run until 1978, has been sponsored by the National Heart and Lung Institute. Proceeding at nine research hospitals and university centers throughout the United States, the study has treated over 150 patients for acute respiratory failure and some have been supported with an artificial lung for up to three weeks. According to the April 1975 *Scientific American,* "the artificial lung may soon join the list of dependable man-made . . . replacements for malfunctioning human organs."

Bionic Heart

When age or disease affects the heart and makes its rhythms irregular or slower than the normal seventy or so beats a minute, the result is inadequate blood supply to the body. In the past this defect was treated by injecting hormonal stimulants directly into the heart, but this treatment was after the fact and often a person with erratic heartbeat died before receiving aid.

The idea for building a device that would send out electric pulses to stimulate the sino-atrial area of the heart and thus regulate its pace first occurred to Dr. A. S. Hyman, director of the Witkin Foundation for the Prevention of Heart Disease, in 1928. Yet it was thirty-one years before the first implantation of an artificial pacemaker took place, for new technological tools had to be devised first. Many of the inert materials used in the pacemaker—epoxy, Silastic, stainless steel, titanium—did not become available until the early 1950s as a consequence of developments in the space program. The same was true of the mercury battery, a long-lasting electrical cell capable of providing current for a minimum of three years. The electronic timer, needed to send out electrical pulses to the heart, was not invented until the early 1950s, after the development of the transistor in 1948 allowed the timer to be miniaturized. The first pacemaker, which weighed only 5 ounces, was implanted in a patient in 1959 by Dr. Samuel Hunter of the University of Minnesota Medical School.

There are drawbacks to pacemakers. Microwave ovens have been known to interfere with the pulses sent out by the device. Some newer models that activate the heartbeat by beaming radio waves at an imbedded receiver, have accidentally set off burglar alarms in department stores equipped with' electronic theft-control devices. There have also been cases of battery failure—but few fatalities as a result.

Recently, a rechargeable battery has been developed that can be recharged inside the person, obviating the need for a patient to undergo surgery to have a new battery installed. New developments arising out of research on atomic energy have also enabled surgeons to implant a pacemaker in the chest powered by radioactive plutonium. The plutonium, which is placed inside a shielded lead container and covered with inert plastic, can power the unit for ten years or more.

But in spite of great surgical and bionic advances, Americans still die of heart attacks at the rate of over 500,000 per year. What is needed, obviously, is a fully functioning bionic heart, and at centers all over the country researchers are competing to be first with a device. Teams such as those headed by De Bakey at Baylor College of Medicine, Kolff at the University of Utah, Cooley at the Texas Heart Institute in Houston, and Tetsuzo Akutsu at the University of Mississippi publish volumes of progress reports each year.

So far researchers throughout the world have tested over fifty different types of prototype bionic hearts with varying degrees of success. There are two main problems in the creation of a bionic heart. First, there is a need for an implantable pump which can take care of all the body's circulatory needs without damaging the blood. Second, there is need for the miniaturization of a suitable power

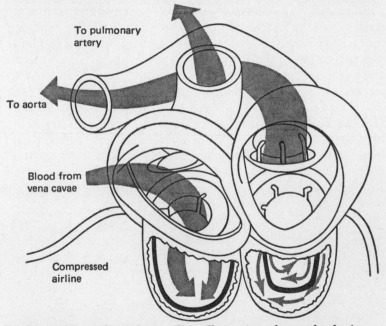

The Kolff artificial heart. This illustration shows the basic design present in most artificial hearts for pumping blood through the body. The Kolff version is driven by compressed air through lines which pass out of the body cavity to air cylinders or to an air pump. Other versions of the artificial heart are driven by electricity or by a small nuclear reactor.

supply. Still, great progress has been made since the first artificial heart was implanted in a dog in 1957 by Akutsu and Kolff. One index of the advances made is the longer survival time in experimental animals implanted with bionic hearts; the first dog lived only 1½ hours, but by 1974 a calf had survived twenty-eight days.

The calf was the recipient of a bionic heart, devised by Kolff and his associates, which was powered by radioactive plutonium-238. In this prototype, which weighed about 4 pounds, the plutonium generated electricity which then powered a gas-driven self-contained Stirling piston engine. Because the Stirling engine was self-contained, there were no waste products. Attached to the engine were flexible drive shafts and gears which in turn powered the heart pump. The entire unit was covered with silicone rubber and the radioactive power source was shielded with lead. When the calf died twenty-eight days after the implantation, it was determined that a blood clot had formed, possibly as a result of pump-induced blood damage, and interfered with the function of the pump.

Despite the problems in developing the nuclear heart, Dr. Lee Smith of Kolff's group said in 1975 that he expected the device to be used in humans within two or three years, that the operation would be so simple that the patients would be up in a day or two, and that the heart would require no maintenance for ten years.

Another research team, headed by Baylor's De Bakey, has come up with a device that consists of one flexible, woven Dacron bag inside another one. The internal bag has Starr-Edwards valves, and after it fills with blood the external bag surrounding it is filled with air. The air pressure that is then exerted on the internal bag forces the blood out into the blood vessels. Theoretically, this type of squeeze-action pump will not damage the blood and this makes it a highly desirable type of pump. So far, however, the De Bakey group has not produced an implantable power source to run their bionic heart, and all preliminary tests on animals have been undertaken with the aid of an elaborate external air pump system that runs the heart via tubes. Among other problems, this arrangement, with tubes running into the body, drastically increases the chances for infection.

A third device which shows some promise is a "beatless" heart developed by a research team at Bio-Medicus, Inc., of Minnetonka,

Minnesota. Since it provides a constant flow of blood, rather than a pumped pulse, it may prove to be far less damaging to the blood than other forms of hearts. But it will be a long time before it is ready to be tested on humans, and so far it has not even been used to completely replace the heart of an experimental animal.

No one knows exactly how long it will take to create an implantable heart, or even if one can be built. The pacemaker took thirty-one years from inception to the creation of a functional unit, and the heart-lung machine took twenty years. The bionic heart is much more complex than either of these, yet substantial progress has been made in the less than twenty years since the first model was produced. As Dr. J. C. Norman of the Texas Heart Institute put it in 1974, "we have slow, continuous progress each year, and I would underline that we have selected the most difficult area, in terms of the totally implantable heart." Yet despite all the difficulties, says Norman, "the future is bright."

The development of artificial replacements for damaged body parts is one of the fastest growing areas of medical research. All over the world scientists are seeking to miniaturize components and create fully functional implants. In addition to those we have talked about, there are "artificial intestines," which provide nutrient infusions for those who, because of disease or surgery, are incapable of intestinal digestion; implantable pumps and capsules for patients needing continual medication; and various kinds of cardiac-assist devices that we have not described. We do not want to mislead the reader into thinking that there is now available a spare part for *every* component of the body; considerable research and testing must be done in many areas. But the work goes forward, and one can visualize a nearly complete bionic body at some point in the future. Except, one would think, for the brain.

THE BIONIC BRAIN

There will always be difficult, dangerous, and unpleasant jobs: working with radioactive materials, undersea mining, space probes, and the like. What if, then, we were able to control a fully bionic body—a robot, actually—from a distance, using our brains to "think" its every move?

This science-fiction idea is not as farfetched as it seems. Since 1973, the Advanced Research Projects Agency of the Pentagon, under a million-dollar program, has been studying ways to connect a computer to a person's EEG (electroencephalograph) signals, or brain waves. The purpose of the agency's developing mind-reading machines to show whether a person is fatigued, daydreaming, or baffled is military, of course: to warn a pilot that his mind is wandering, to enable a gunner to bypass his body's motor system and fire by cerebral reflex, to tell interpreters of aerial photos taken for reconnaissance purposes—who must remember details from photos taken previously—as to when their "photographic memory" (which theoretically every person has) is operating at peak performance.

The program is being carried out by several scientists working under contract to the Pentagon. The lead institution is the University of Illinois, but others include MIT, UCLA, the University of Rochester, Stanford, and Stanford Research Institute. Neurophysiologist and electrical engineer Lawrence Pinneo of SRI, for instance, has devised a "thinking cap" which picks up the EEGs corresponding to a particular thought and, through a computer, analyzes the current produced by the thought, including how a person perceives colors and shapes and how alert he is. Pinneo's subjects, with electrodes attached to their heads, have also been able to move dots from side to side on a computerized TV screen simply by *thinking*, and have even been able to think an object through a maze. Electrodes may not always be needed. At MIT, researchers are studying magnetic brain waves that can be charted much like those now made from EEG waves. Such magnetic waves could be picked up, perhaps, by a receiver placed close by the head.

At present a massive amount of research is being done on the brain. For example, scientists are studying it to mimic its function in building better computers. There is no telling what form all these research paths will take. "Every technological prediction has been wrong," one scientist maintains. "Who knows what the next century will bring?" Or even, we might add, the next ten years.

What if, facing the certainty of our death, we were able to convey all our thoughts, feelings, and experience to a computer—turn over our entire *persona* to a truly bionic brain—that could store it until such time as it could be transmitted to another human body? Indeed, as we shall see in the next chapter, that other body might even be our own.

6. Cryobiology and Other Low-Temperature Strategies

In 1965, with the publication of *The Promise of Immortality* by Robert Ettinger, the general public first became aware of the concept of cryonic suspension—the quick freezing of the recently dead for revival in the future when the illness that killed them becomes curable. Although much that was claimed about life extension through suspended animation has been attacked by the scientific community, the basic notions of low-temperature life extension are well substantiated by scientific observation and experiment.

One day in April 1975, Warren Churchill, age sixty, a bearded biologist from the University of Wisconsin, set out with two colleagues to conduct a fish survey on the still-icy Lake Wingra, in the cold back country of Wisconsin. While on the lake their boat capsized, and the three men were plunged into the lake's 41-degree water. It was an hour and a half before they were rescued, and when the paramedics arrived, Churchill was not breathing. Moreover, his skin was blue, his heartbeat faint, his blood pressure zero—and his body temperature had dropped to 65 degrees Fahrenheit, 33 degrees below normal.

Although he resumed breathing en route to the hospital, his body temperature dropped even more—to 61 degrees. At the hospital he was placed between two rubber blankets with tubes inside circulating warm fluid, like a large hot water bottle. Still, his shivering—the body's way of generating heat—became so intense that it began to damage his muscles. In order to block the nerve impulses from Churchill's brain that instructed his body to shiver, his physician, Marvin Birnbaum, ordered an injection of curare, a substance also used as nerve poison on the tips of blow-gun darts by Amazonian Indians to kill small game. The injection worked and Churchill survived. Other than shivering-caused soreness in his muscles, which lasted for several months, he showed no ill effects. In spite of his having stopped breathing for so long and the loss of blood pressure, there was no brain damage.

How was this possible? Under normal conditions humans can live only a maximum of five minutes without breathing. Even then the lack of oxygen usually causes irreversible brain damage, destroying memory and intellectual faculties. But with Churchill the 41-degree water so slowed down the rate of his bodily chemical reactions and diminished his body's need for oxygen that his brain escaped this damage.

Churchill's experience dramatically shows that *cold* can help prevent damage to the body similar to that which occurs during aging, when the capacity of the blood to carry oxygen to the brain is reduced.

Metabolism is the chemical reaction in the body that supplies the cells with energy. One factor that greatly influences metabolism is temperature. Higher temperature increases the speed of chemical reactions; lower temperature decreases it. Meat stored at room temperature (about 70 degrees Fahrenheit) will decay within a couple of days, and in desert temperatures (around 90 degrees) in a matter of hours. But meat in a refrigerator at 39 degrees will stay fresh for two weeks, and at 32 degrees in a freezer for six months or so.

Small animals such as mice have very fast metabolic rates; their bodies' chemical reactions occur very quickly. Large animals such as elephants usually have much slower metabolic rates. The reason for this variation is the relationship between body size and skin area. A small animal has much more surface area exposed to the elements, relative to its size, than does a large animal. This fact of animal surface geometry causes small animals to lose body heat much faster than larger animals do, since they have more surface area, in proportion to their weight, through which heat can escape. Animals maintain their body temperature by generating heat during the chemical reactions of metabolism, and small animals therefore must have a faster metabolic rate than larger animals in order to compensate for their greater rate of heat loss. This need for a faster metabolic rate affects every aspect of the small animals' existence. Whereas large animals can exploit food sources such as leaves which provide less energy, small animals must feed on things that quickly supply large quantities of energy, such as high-protein nuts and sugar-rich berries.

The faster metabolic rate of smaller animals also shortens their lives: elephants live up to seventy-seven years, mice live up to three. Smaller animals, with their higher metabolic rates, go through life more quickly and intensely than larger animals do. And their chemical reactions causing breakdown and decay also occur faster.

Humans violate this rule, because we survive much longer than would be expected from our size—longer than the gorilla, for instance, which lives only about forty-five years. Perhaps this is because our more advanced brains have enabled us to exert far better control over our metabolism and so control more efficiently the chemical reactions that lead to aging. Our body chemistry is more efficient and better controlled than that of other animals so that the chemical reactions that cause aging happen at a slower rate. But it could be better. If we could alter our metabolic rates, we might be able to slow the rate of breakdown even further.

TURNING DOWN THE HUMAN THERMOSTAT

According to Roy Walford, a researcher on aging at UCLA, simply lowering the body temperature of humans a few degrees could theoretically greatly extend life span in man. Research by George A. Sacher at the Argonne National Laboratory in Illinois has shown that lowering body temperature has its strongest effect on the last half of life, because that is when the chemical changes leading to bodily decay are speeding up and can therefore be more greatly affected by lowering body temperature.

On simple animals such as fruit flies, says Dr. Bernard Strehler of the Andrus Gerontology Center at the University of Southern California, "a tenfold increase in longevity has been achieved by lowering body temperature, without adversely affecting body function." Lowering body temperatures may not help humans as much as it does fruit flies, but Strehler feels there could still be substantial gain. "A very minor reduction in temperature, about 3 degrees Farenheit," he says, "could well add as much as thirty years to human life."

Strehler has pointed out that drugs already exist that can reduce temperature by the requisite amount. Barbiturates, for example, are known to inhibit the ability of the hypothalamus to accurately regulate body temperature. (This is why the combination of alcohol—which can cause the body to become flushed and therefore lose heat rapidly—and barbiturates can be fatal through a loss of body heat so rapid that the heart stops.) There are also chemicals that have effects similar to barbiturates, such as norepinephrine, which is normally found in our bodies in small amounts.

However, it may not be necessary to subject ourselves to drugs in order to lower our body temperatures. Strehler says that Australian aborigines have the ability to suppress the reflex that causes shivering, our body's heat-producing reaction to cold. With this ability to suppress our body's response to diminished body temperature, we can lower our body temperature while still remaining healthy.

One way to learn this is through biofeedback. By hooking volunteers up to a sensitive biofeedback machine which reports, either by sound or visually, when they have achieved the desired internal state, a number of researchers have been able to teach people to vary their skin temperatures by just thinking about it. Edward Taub, a psychologist at the Institute for Behavioral Research in Silver Springs, Maryland, has taught people to vary the skin temperature of their hands and feet by as much as 15 degrees, with only an hour's practice.

Such a lowering of body temperature would not really be an abnormal state. Everyone undergoes a slight daily decline in body temperature—perhaps as much as half a degree—during sleep. We would simply be augmenting a natural process by causing our temperatures to fall a few degrees instead of half a degree. All cases of carefully controlled lowering of human body temperature—whether done during surgical procedures, as therapy for disease, or as experiments—have shown that such a lowering has no lasting ill effects.

Taking a few pills, or a series of biofeedback lessons, and getting used to a slightly colder body could enable people to live a good deal longer, perhaps even enabling them to undergo long periods of nearly dormant, and therefore ageless, resting such as happens with hibernating animals.

COLD TREATMENT

The marmot, a large rodent living in the western United States, has a metabolism that operates so fast that during periods of normal activity its heart beats 200 times a minute (ours beats about seventy). In hibernation, however, the marmot's energy and metabolism requirements diminish to the point where its heart needs to beat only *five* times a minute. Because of its decreased need for oxygen, its rate of breathing also diminishes drastically. Hibernation also diminishes the need for food. Some hibernating animals let their body temperatures fall until they are within a couple of degrees of the environmental temperature—often within two or three degrees of freezing. During this period, all their biological processes slow down dramatically and they expend almost no energy.

The life extension benefits of hibernation may be seen when the bat, a hibernating animal, is compared with the shrew, a non-hibernator of about the same size. The shrew is a small, furry animal similar to a mole and lives in nearly every country in the world. Shrews have no way of reducing metabolism or body temperature except slightly during sleep. Bats, however, can apparently reduce their metabolism to 1/150th that of their normal activity. The result: the bat lives twenty years or more; the shrew lives fourteen to seventeen months.

Hibernation not only seems to extend life in some animals but also to slow disease. In hibernation a transplanted cancer does not seem to kill the animal, although on awakening the tumor again will begin to grow. Hibernating animals suffer only localized damage from x-ray radiation and are resistant to plant and bacterial poisons. Indeed, hibernating animals can recover from plague and parasitic diseases, in many instances without treatment.

There are three reasons why low-temperature hibernation makes animals immune to some diseases. First, many organisms, such as plague bacteria and parasites, cannot live in environments with temperatures much lower than that of normal human body temperature (98.6 degrees). Second, tissue damage (such as that done by x-rays) does not happen in a hibernating animal as much as it does in an animal at normal temperature because hibernation, with its low metabolism, keeps the damaging molecular breakdown localized. Third, tumors, which have extremely fast metabolisms and generally thrive at higher body temperatures, remain dormant during hibernation.

In the 1950s, medical researchers began to try to induce hypothermia, an artificial state of low body temperature, in humans. Hypothermia was so effective, according to Vojin and Pava Popovic of the Emory University School of Medicine, who were among the first to use the procedure, that it had applications in cases of hypoxia (lack of oxygen), ischemia (lack of blood), asphyxia (lack of air), shock, burns, poisoning, and in heart and brain surgery.

Early in the century, Sutherland Simpson and Percy T. Herring, two physiologists at the University of Edinburgh, began to try to induce hibernation in monkeys. They found that at about 77 degrees the animal was insensitive to pain and incapable of being aroused—it was, in fact, narcotized by cold. It was possible, they concluded, to maintain a monkey in this condition for some time.

Artificial hibernation was not attempted on humans, however, until 1951, when at the Hospital Vaugirard in Paris anesthesiologist Pierre Huguenard placed a middle-aged man, one whose heart valves needed surgical repair, into "cold sleep." At the time of this experiment, the heart-lung machine had not been fully developed, and the only way a brain or heart surgeon could keep his patient alive and prevent decay while stopping his blood flow was to reduce the metabolism by lowering the body temperature.

Once anesthetized, the patient was injected with a "lytic cocktail" (from the Greek lysis, meaning to loosen or release) containing drugs such as chlorpromazine and barbiturates, to stop the shiver resulting from the lowered body temperature and also prevent his body from speeding up its metabolism to produce heat. The patient was then covered with a cold blanket—a rubber sheet with tubes inside connected to a pump that circulated ice water.

When the patient's body temperature was decreased to 86 degrees, his chest was opened, his heart stopped with an injection of a muscle-relaxing drug, and the surgeon clamped the major blood vessels to the heart. This resulted in a "blood-free field," a heart without blood, which allowed quick repair of the damaged heart valve. During the cold sleep, the patient's metabolism was diminished by nearly 40 percent, and there was no damage to the brain and other organs from lack of oxygen. The cold sleep extended the length of time a surgeon could operate from a few minutes to two hours.

With the advent of the heart-lung machine in the early 1950s, cold sleep was abandoned for heart operations, and today cold sleep is used mainly on those undergoing certain brain operations. It is also used on children, whose blood is more susceptible to damage by the heart-lung machine. However, Huguenard's technique has been greatly refined and is now a routine procedure. Patients can be cooled more deeply than was possible a few years ago. Emory's Pava Popovic believes people can survive a body temperature of about 39 degrees Fahrenheit, only seven degrees above freezing.

Huguenard's technique has never been used on humans for more than a few hours, but it may be possible to lower a person's body temperature for longer amounts of time by chemically short-circuiting the body's temperature-sensing nerves or blocking the reception of the temperature impulses by the hypothalmus. This might allow the body to keep its temperature on nearly the same level as that of the environment—which means that a low-temperature environment would decrease a person's biological activity.

Like bats, humans may be able to spend their nights in hibernation instead of sleep, according to Dr. William Dement of the Stanford University School of Medicine, perhaps the foremost researcher on sleep. If temperature were lowered beyond the normal point, he says, there would probably be a further increase in depth of sleep. Drugs lowering body temperature a few degrees could bring on a state of "natural" cold sleep, and diminishing temperature only a few degrees might be enough to retard aging during the third of our lives we spend sleeping.

LONG-TERM COLD SLEEP

Some animals hibernate for six to eight months a year. If we were to take advantage of this state, then, we should also be able to sleep for days or months at a time. This would require two important modifications of the present procedures used to bring about cold sleep in humans. One problem is supplying food to the body, the other is in administering the drugs to keep the body from reacting to the cold.

Animals that hibernate, such as the hedgehog, store up enormous amounts of fat in their bodies to serve as food so that they do not have to wake up and eat. The fat may increase their weight as much as three times. Up to 3 percent of the body weight may be made up of brown fat, a special kind of oily, dark fat that remains liquid at low temperatures and can produce a large amount of body heat when utilized as food. Brown fat is thought to be crucial in keeping animals from freezing during hibernation. Humans, in contrast, do not have very much fat stored in their bodies—usually not more than 10 percent of the body weight—and less than a thirtieth the amount of brown fat that hibernating animals have.

Still, to gain weight in stored fat, all we have to do is eat more food than we need. And compared to a small hibernator like a dormouse, we need to gain less weight in order to stay alive for the same amount of time because we have a lower metabolic rate. Research on rats has shown that their level of brown fat can be increased by exposure to cold, and NASA consultant and futurist Robert Prehoda believes it may be possible to increase the amount of brown fat in humans with a carefully controlled program of exposure to low temperature. In fact, humans normally have more brown fat when they are born, which is why infants may be more resistant to cold than adults are.

The drawback to putting on extra fat, however, is that it puts a severe strain on our bodies—obese people do not live as long as thinner people—and we might have to put on up to two-thirds of our body weight in stored fat in order to be able to spend several months asleep. Also, many people suffer from an inherited inability to process excess fat properly, so that it can clog up their blood vessels, leading to heart attacks and strokes. Thus, other ways of providing food for people in a cold sleep may be better.

One such method is to feed people intravenously during the cold sleep state. In 1968 Dr. Stanley J. Dudrick, at the University of Texas Medical School in Houston, perfected a technique of total intravenous nutrition which could promote normal metabolism in people for prolonged periods of time. Dudrick's solution contains all nutrients—proteins, sugars, fats, vitamins, and minerals—needed to keep a person alive without any other source of food. Administration of the intravenous solution, which is now a routine procedure, is usually added directly into the subclavian vein, the large blood vessel running across the base of the neck. In 1974, a patient was continuously fed by this method for over seven months and it may be possible to extend it longer. Some research is needed to determine the effect of total intravenous feeding on people whose metabolic rate is depressed, as would be the case in cold sleep, but the technique shows promise.

The second major problem with making long-term cold sleep feasible is controlling the drugs used to prevent the body from reacting to the cold. These drugs, such as chlorpromazine, have a strong effect on the brain. Too much of any one of them could depress the nerve cells of the brain to the point where the brain could not keep the body alive—it would simply lose control of functions like breathing and heartbeat. Also, no one knows what effects these drugs have on people over long periods of time.

Further, the drugs need to be administered in exactly the right amounts at the right time, or results can be deadly. This means that the blood of cold sleepers would need constant monitoring to keep the drug levels safe. A device that allows researchers to remove blood samples whenever they wish was developed in 1956 by Dr. Joseph W. Still at the George Washington University School of Medicine. Still implanted a small plastic tube inside the aorta of rats and left it there for over ten months with no apparent ill effects. The tube was left in the aorta at all times, and the end outside the body was clamped shut to prevent leakage. When a blood sample was desired, Still simply released the clamp. He was also able to introduce drugs into the rats through the tube whenever he wanted. Still's technique was adapted to studying the metabolism of hibernating animals, and has been used successfully for almost twenty years in hibernation research at Harvard Medical School. Adapting the technique to monitoring blood and introducing drugs in humans in cold sleep should likewise be possible.

None of the obstacles in the way to achieving prolonged cold sleep are insurmountable. Most of the solutions involve going from techniques already available and perfected to alterations necessary for use in cold sleepers. The ultimate promise of cold sleep has a far more distant future.

THE CRYONICS MOVEMENT

On January 12, 1967, a seventy-three-year-old man was dying of lung cancer in a small convalescent home in the town of Glendale near Los Angeles. At his bedside were several members of the Los Angeles Cryonics Society, a nonprofit organization whose purpose was to learn how to freeze people at the time of death, in hopes they could later be reanimated if a cure for the particular cause of death were found.

The man was James H. Bedford, a former psychology professor at Glendale City College who had amassed a considerable fortune in land investments. He was also interested in cryonics and had donated $200,000 toward setting up the first cryonics laboratory in Los Angeles.

At 6:30 P.M. his condition was grave and he began gasping for breath. Shortly afterward his personal physician, Dr. B. Renault Able, who was also interested in the possibilities of cryonics and low-temperature storage, pronounced him dead.

Able quickly connected Bedford's body to a heart-lung machine, flooding it with nutrients and oxygen, in an attempt to keep the brain from degenerating. At the same time he injected Bedford's body with heparin, a chemical that prevents blood from clotting. Then, with the help of Dr. Dante Brunol, a member of the Los Angeles Cryonics Society, Able attempted to freeze the body as fast as possible. Dimethyl sulfoxide (DSFO), a chemical "antifreeze" that prevents ice crystals from forming in living tissue when it is frozen, was injected into Bedford's bloodstream. At the same time, the body was packed in dry ice. Slowly the temperature of the body was lowered to near freezing and then the heart-lung machine was shut off. By 2:00 A.M. Bedford's body temperature stood at 100 degrees below zero, the temperature of dry ice.

A seven-foot-long, "cryogenic storage capsule," designed by a California engineer, was brought into the room. Made of polished stainless steel, the capsule was constructed with double walls, like a Thermos bottle, to act as insulation to maintain the cold.

Bedford's frozen body was wrapped in aluminum foil, placed inside the capsule, and the hatch was screwed closed. The chamber was then filled with liquid nitrogen, a liquified gas with a temperature of about 320 degrees below zero, and within seconds Bedford's tissues had become as brittle as glass. A few days later, the capsule containing the body of Bedford was flown to a facility in Arizona to be stored against the day when a cure for terminal cancer might be found—and also a way to reanimate dead tissue.

Bedford had always been a quiet man who abhorred publicity. He had given his money and time toward furthering various kinds of scientific research and, in an effort to advance the science of low-temperature storage, had volunteered to be the first person to undergo "cryonic suspension." Although members of the Cryonics Society estimated that his body could be preserved for several hundred million years without any deterioration, Bedford himself was well aware that the chances of his own reanimation some time in the distant future were not good. He wanted his own cryonic suspension to proceed with dignity and without publicity.

Robert C. W. Ettinger, a professor of physics at Upstate Michigan Junior College and another exponent of cryonics, on the other hand, is considerably less reserved and publicity-shy about its prospects. "Won't you feel a fool if you are one of the last mortals to die?" he has asked rhetorically. "Won't you be ridiculous if you are one of the last humans thrown on the scrap-heap of history? . . . Won't you be chagrined when we dance on your grave? Will you hold still for this? Will you hold still? Will you?"

Ettinger founded the Michigan Cryonics Society shortly after publication of his book *The Promise of Immortality* in 1965. When through associates he heard of Bedford's death, he and other "cryonicists" caught a plane for Los Angeles. There, after learning the circumstances of Bedford's historic freezing, he called a press conference to announce to the world what had happened.

As a result of a press release put out by Ettinger which listed the names of all the observers present, it was only a short time before one of them told the press Bedford's name. Within hours Bedford's family, his physician, and the observers were beseiged by television and print journalists hard after news and pictures. Ettinger appeared on radio and TV talk shows all over the world, and became famous presenting a single scientific experiment as a surefire way to immortality.

The result, ironically, was that the Bedford family became so distressed over the unexpected and misleading publicity that they began litigation to withdraw the funds Bedford had left his foundation for cryobiological research, even though some experiments had already been started with Bedford's money. In short, R. C. W. Ettinger's zeal may have closed the doors of perhaps one of the best equipped laboratories for the study of cryobiology.

Ettinger says he bases his ideas on contacts with numerous researchers, such as those belonging to the worldwide Society for Cryobiology, whom he has asked whether it would be possible to freeze a body so carefully that it could be stored indefinitely. Most such researchers were simply measuring the effects of cold on living tissues, yet they told Ettinger that they believed at some time in the distant future it might be possible to freeze a person and later revive him without damaging the delicate cellular structures that enable life to happen. Ettinger took these cautious statements as a scientific mandate, and proceeded to begin promoting cryonics as "the greatest promist . . . of all history, not excepting that of nuclear energy."

Ettinger's faith in the abilities of future doctors is so great that he even suggests people's brains ought to be sliced into sections at the time of death, so as to quicken the freezing process. Robot surgeons of the future, he says, "working twenty-four hours a day for decades, even centuries, will tenderly restore the frozen brains, cell by cell, or even molecule by molecule, in critical areas."

Since Bedford's experiment, an estimated fifty people have been frozen by cryonics societies throughout the United States. The method of freezing differs little from that first attempted on Bedford in 1967. Currently, a person's body is packed in dry ice at the time of death, drained of blood, filled with glycerol and DMSO (dimethylsulfoxide), an antifreezing and -penetrating agent, to prevent ice crystals from forming within the individual cells, and then stored at minus 320 degrees Fahrenheit.

Bodies are "buried" in cryonics cemeteries, which employ auxillary methods of powering the refrigeration units to keep a person frozen even in the event of a power failure (though not necessarily nuclear attack). According to Trans-Time, a Berkeley, California, for-profit cryonics company, decay that would take "1 second at normal body temperatures would take more than 30 trillion years at the [minus 320 degree] temperature at which patients are stored."

The thing one must remember about the cryonics freeze-wait-reanimate plan is that the person is *dead*. If the body is to be thawed out at some time in the future when the cause of death can be cured by medical science, doctors then must not only be able to retroactively cure the disease but also be able to revive the dead. At present, reactivating dead matter is nowhere near possible, for the damage that occurs to cells, even after only a few minutes of death, is so vast as to be irreparable. At death, at least a trillion molecules break down, which means that Ettinger's robot surgeons of the future, even if they repaired a molecule a second, would still take 20,000 years. Moreover, today after the heart stops, at normal temperatures it takes less than five minutes for the brain to perish, in which time so many brain cells break down that all memory and thought are lost. Once this happens, there is no way to bring back those intellectual capabilities. Unless specific ways to rebuild the brain were found, reanimating a person who was frozen just five minutes after death would only serve to reanimate the mind of a vegetable. In addition, at death the enzymes in the pancreas first destroy the pancreas itself, bursting the cells in it and the surrounding areas. Unless freezing is simultaneous with death, most reanimated persons would have to be provided with at least an artificial pancreas.

Another problem with freeze-reanimate is that people are 70 percent water. When water freezes, it becomes tiny, sharp ice crystals that do irreparable damage inside living tissues. Frostbite is an example of living tissue that freezes; ice crystals damage the delicate membranes surrounding the cells and cause their vital chemicals to ooze out when the cells thaw. There is, as yet, no way to heal a cell after it has been damaged by such freezing.

The kinds of antifreezes used by most cryonic societies, such as DMSO and glycerol, may be ineffective against such cellular damage. John Farrant, of the National Institute of Medical Research in London, a longtime leader in cryobiological research, says DMSO has been successful as an antifreeze down to as low as 100 degrees below freezing. Even at this low temperature, however, some metabolic and biological processes would still occur. Between 100 and 200 degrees below freezing, says Dr. Armand Karnow, Jr., an expert on freezing of cells and organs at the Medical College of Georgia, cells remain stable for only a few months; beyond that they undergo appreciable aging. But Farrant still feels that his procedure will allow cells to be safely frozen without ice crystal formation to as low as −320 degrees, and so it "will form the basis for the successful freezing, storage, and thawing of tissues which require 100 percent cell survival in order to function." Karnow also feels this procedure seems to offer bright prospects for cryopreservation or preservation by freezing. This conclusion was partly borne out by Donald Whittingham of Cambridge University who protected mouse embryos with DMSO by freezing and keeping them at 320 degrees below zero for as long as seven months. When the embryos were revived, even after more than half a year, nearly a third were able to recover and develop into healthy adult mice. So far, however, what works for embryos has not worked for living mice—none have survived such freezing.

All these problems must be solved before freezing, but the greatest problem is how to anticipate what to do *after* freezing. How can a large, complex organism like a human being be thawed out? To be successful, the thawing must be uniform and quick. For instance, if a brain thaws while the body is still frozen, the brain will quickly die because the frozen arteries will not immediately supply it with oxygen. The capillaries would still be frozen shut at the moment blood was reintroduced and would make the transfused blood clot. The problem is to develop a way to evenly and instantly thaw the body.

One way is to use microwaves to thaw frozen organs gently, evenly, and quickly. Experimenting with dog kidneys frozen at 4 degrees below zero, Ronald Dietzman of the University of Minnesota was able to quickly thaw the organs in microwave units similar in design to home microwave ovens. Dietzman perfused the dog kidneys with DMSO antifreeze, thawed the kidneys, and then reimplanted them into the dogs they were originally taken from—and the reimplanted organs gained complete function within a week.

Warming an organism with microwaves can be extremely tricky. An animal's cold spots can be beamed with microwaves to cause the spots to thaw. But a slight misadjustment in the setting of the machine can result in what is called "thermal runaway"—and instead of an electronically warmed and thawed body, there is a thoroughly cooked one. Dietzman's technique is so experimental it cannot be performed on people or even complex animals because each type of tissue and organ has different rates of freezing and thawing. Still, Karnow believes microwaves are the key to successful thawing of frozen tissues.

THE POSSIBILITIES FOR SUSPENDED ANIMATION

Even if the problems inherent in freezing and thawing are worked out, it is unlikely that anybody so far frozen by the cryonics societies will be brought back to life. The procedure used probably amounts to little more than an ice pack on a dead body. No animal—not even fish from the almost frozen waters of the Arctic—has ever been frozen and thawed successfully, even with the use of antifreezes such as glycerol and DMSO. To give a future doctor the chance to revive a frozen patient, extremely precise methods of thawing and freezing must be used—methods much more precise than those the cryonics people have so far employed. Dr. Audrey U. Smith, of the National Institute for Medical Research in London, England, the first researcher to use an antifreeze to successfully freeze and thaw individual cells, states that the "established data on resuscitating ice-cold and frozen animals and man after periods of cardiac and respiratory arrest . . . do not support the idea that human beings can hope to be resurrected years after their bodies have been frozen and stored at low temperatures after death."

Years of research by cryobiologists have presented a reasonably detailed picture of what must be done if freezing is to become a usable life-extension method. The techniques are based on those used to freeze cells such as blood and sperm, or those being tried in preserving organs. In addition, the use of xenon gas as an antifreeze, which theoretically may be useful in the freezing and thawing of human bodies, has also been proposed. But more than new kinds of freezing techniques are required. Most importantly, a person must be frozen *before* death.

Of course, any researcher who froze a living person today would under present laws be arrested for murder, but let us see how the procedure might work. The body of a living person is capable of a great deal of adjustment to changing conditions, through the action of individual cells, through the release of hormones, and through the regulatory role of the brain. The body of a dead person has no such regulatory abilities, and therefore drastic measures are necessary immediately after death to keep the body from degenerating while freezing is being attempted. At death a body will start destroying itself through the action of uncontrolled digestive enzymes and other chemicals which were carefully regulated during life. Microorganisms of all kinds immediately start growing on the body and begin breaking it down. Cooling the body and injecting drugs such as heparin slows down these destructive processes but does not stop them. They do not cease until the body is frozen at a temperature below that of dry ice (about 97 degrees below zero). These drugs and chemicals may also interfere in some way with the smoothness of the freezing process. Death stops the metabolic processes that maintain and store human memory in the cells of the brain; if some of these molecules are destroyed before freezing, there is the possibility that, on thawing, the brain would be blank. Finally, artificial procedures to maintain and protect the body of a dead person while it thaws present the same problems as when it is frozen—that is, the body is unable to regulate its reactions or protect its organs and cells so that thawing could cause severe damage. After death, obviously, speed is an absolute necessity, and that can mean that either the freezing will be delayed too long, if a person dies far from the necessary facilities, or that mistakes will occur because of haste. For these reasons, the revival of a frozen corpse, we believe, is impossible.

If a person were frozen while alive, then the natural regulatory processes of the body could compensate during the early stages of cooling to help the body over the initial shock. In addition, the still-beating heart could be used to help circulate antifreezes through the body, obviating the need for pumps to do the job, which can cause damage to the cells and organs, as sometimes occurs when a heart-lung pump is used. By starting freezing when a person is alive, the individual's own regulatory systems could protect the molecules of memory until cooling had progressed to a point where they were no longer in danger of being destroyed. Finally, freezing a living person would be better because it would assist the thawing process if the person's body could start operating as thawing proceeded. In a living person, the heart could be started after the body had been thawed sufficiently and the blood vessels cleared, which would insure an adequate blood supply to the organs. Also, the body's regulatory processes could help protect the body from any metabolic imbalances due to thawing.

The process of cooling and freezing would begin, according to Robert Prehoda, by lightly anesthetizing the person and then fitting him with a shunt, a tube sewn into the artery of his arm, similar to ones used by kidney machine patients. This shunt would be used to take blood from the individual and run it through a refrigerator-like device which would cool the blood slowly, allowing the body to gradually adjust to the drop in temperature. This would also produce an even cooling, which is necessary to prevent tissue damage. The person's body temperature would be lowered very slowly, perhaps at the rate of 10 degrees an hour. At the same time, the blood could be slowly replaced with a special cold-resistant, artificial fluorocarbon "blood" (not now available), which would have a lower freezing point than real blood, and would allow circulation to proceed at a lower temperature than if real blood were used. The synthetic blood would also permit lower freezing temperatures to be used and therefore would reduce the chance of ice crystal formation inside of the cells. In addition, the fluorocarbon blood would be able to carry more oxygen at low temperatures than would real blood, and thereby help protect the body cells from oxygen starvation.

After about three hours of this, when the body temperature was down to about 60 degrees, the kidneys and heart would no longer be able to function normally. The person would then be hooked up to a kidney machine and a heart-lung machine, and all the "blood"—now completely composed of fluorocarbons—would be pumped and filtered by these machines.

The cooling process would proceed, slowly and regularly, degree by degree, after the person was attached to the life-support machines. At the same time, xenon gas would be dissolved into the synthetic blood. The use of xenon—a rare, chemically inert gas related to neon—was first suggested by Prehoda because he believes xenon in large quantities might significantly modify ice crystal formation without causing damage. According to Prehoda, xenon forms protective "socks" around the complex molecules which make up the cells, and these chemically inert socks could protect the life-sustaining compounds from damage during freezing.

As the temperature of the person was lowered toward freezing, the atmospheric pressure of the special airtight freezing room would be increased by pumping in a mixture of both xenon and oxygen gas. Because of the xenon and oxygen atmospheric pressure, the body could be cooled to around 100 degrees below zero without freezing and ice crystal formation. Then the pressure would be quickly dropped, releasing extra atmospheric pressure, which would have the effect of quickly turning the patient's body into a solid frozen mass, still without any ice crystal formation. The frozen body could then be placed in a special container, similar to a Thermos bottle, which would be surrounded by liquid nitrogen. The body would now be protected and frozen, immune from all the effects of time, and could stay that way without any biological change. According to the Russian cryobiologist L. K. Lozina-Lozinskii, for a frozen person "the factor of time no longer has the same significance that it has for the living object in an active state and it may be assumed that . . . whole organisms may remain in a viable state for an indefinite period of time."

When it was time to thaw the person, the body would be removed from the storage container and placed in an airtight freezing room. The room would be quickly filled with xenon and oxygen to increase the atmospheric pressure to prevent ice crystals from forming at about 32 degrees during the thawing process. Microwaves would be aimed at the body to gently and evenly thaw it. As the temperature of the body rose above the freezing point of fluorocarbon blood, heart-lung and kidney machines would be connected, with the addition of a warming machine to slowly bring the body back to normal temperature. As this occurred, the artificial blood would be removed, in stages, and replaced with human blood— possibly the patient's own blood, removed years before and also frozen. By the time the body temperature reached 60 degrees, the heart-lung, kidney, and warming machines could be removed and the person's own heart would be electrically stimulated into again pumping his own blood through the body. The individual could then be prepared for surgery or treatment for whatever condition he was suffering from prior to his being frozen.

We are still a considerable distance away from all this—indeed we may never reach this goal. To date, no animal has been completely frozen and revived. Still, Prehoda believes the future may offer us the possibility "of permitting man to be preserved indefinitely in a state of suspended animation at extremely low temperatures."

Drastic procedures such as freezing humans in order to prolong life may not be necessary, however, if research on the biology of aging proves as promising as it seems. Some of the most successful research on aging is presented in the next chapter.

7. The Biology of Aging

Some day, says Yale biologist Arthur W. Galston, we may well have an "antiaging cocktail" to slow or reverse aging. Because age causes many different kinds of cellular changes, it is unlikely, he says, that "any single elixer will be able to retard all these degenerative changes." The antiaging cocktail, Galston believes, will have to be a complicated, multicomponent fountain-of-youth concoction consisting of a combination of drugs, hormones, and enzymes. To understand why this mix will probably be necessary will require our traveling at least five roads of theory about aging. And to understand them, we must first examine how cells live, age, and die, for it is in our cells that aging begins.

THE LIFE OF CELLS

The cell, the smallest unit that has all the properties associated with life, reproduces itself through a splitting process called division, the result of which is two cells. All cells come from preexisting cells.

The one cell of a chicken embryo divides to make two, the two divide to make four, and so on, until the billions of cells that make up the newly hatched chick are produced. And the same process occurs in humans to make the trillion cells of an adult from a single cell, the fertilized egg. Each cell parcels out its various chemical components into two equal parts by splitting down the middle during division, so that the two new cells, although smaller than the "parent" cell, at first, still contain all the necessary materials to carry on metabolism (the chemical reactions that supply the cell with energy). Both cells are surrounded by a tough membrane regulating inflow of nutrients and output of wastes.

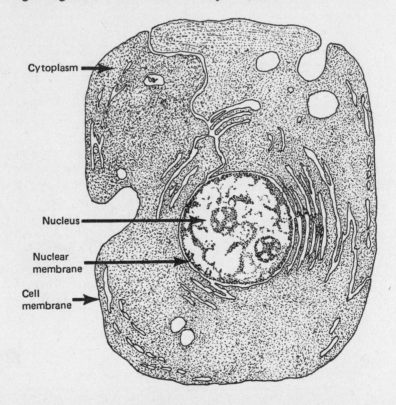

A typical animal cell.

Cells are made up of several major classes of chemicals called organic molecules ("organic" means pertaining to life)—sugars, fats, proteins, and nucleic acids. All these large, complex molecules play a special role in the life of a cell. Sugars provide the energy necessary to keep cells functioning. Fats serve as storage molecules in cells, a kind of reserve form of energy that can be utilized if not enough sugar is present. Fats also make up part of the membrane surrounding each cell. Proteins, which likewise make up part of the membrane (and which, along with fats, regulate the movement of substances into and out of the cell), are also found inside the cell itself in the cytoplasm, a mixture of water and chemicals. Some of these internal proteins, called enzymes, act to speed up the many chemical reactions of metabolism, which would otherwise occur too slowly to sustain the life of the cell. Nucleic acids are found largely in a special structure inside each cell called the nucleus, a semispherical body usually located approximately in the center of each cell. There are two main types of nucleic acids—deoxyribonucleic acid, or DNA, and ribonucleic acid, or RNA. Both are large, lengthy, complex chains of atoms.

In the 1940s a group of bacteriologists headed by Oswald T. Avery, at the Rockefeller Institute in New York, showed that DNA is the molecule that carries the information necessary to specify all the chemical reactions and structures of a cell. Avery's group demonstrated that DNA is, in a way, the force that directs life, growth, and division of cells.

The discovery of the central role of DNA in cellular metabolism touched off an international race to discover the exact structure of DNA and how that structure allows DNA to govern the chemical processes in the cell. The race was won in 1953 by two young molecular biologists working at Cambridge University in England, Francis Crick and James D. Watson. Watson and Crick showed that DNA directs the metabolism, structure, and division of a cell by producing RNA, which acts as a supervisor molecule to direct the manufacture of proteins. The proteins in turn drive the cell's metabolism, form much of the cell's structure, and help regulate cell division. When a cell divides, the two "daughter" cells, as they are called by geneticists, besides getting a complement of proteins, fats, and sugars, also receive a vital complement of DNA to direct their metabolism and growth.

To the biologists of the late nineteenth century, cells seemed wonderful and mysterious. When they examined single-celled organisms, such as amoebas, they found that the cells seemed immortal as long as they could grow and divide and as long as they could avoid microscopic predators. During the 1920s and 1930s the experiments of biologists such as Alexis Carrel seemed to indicate that single cells were indeed immortal, and that aging and death were a function only of large combinations of cells such as occur in humans. Carrel, in fact, was able to isolate cells from complex organisms such as chickens, and those cells seemingly carried on metabolism and continued to divide years after the chickens they came from had died. But Carrel was proved wrong.

THE HAYFLICK EXPERIMENTS: THE GENETIC LIMITS TO LIFE

In 1961, Dr. Leonard Hayflick, then of Stanford University, discovered in the course of doing cancer research that human cells growing in a culture (a chemical formulation that supplies them with the energy and nutrients needed for them to live) could divide only a limited number of times before all their descendants aged and died. The number of divisions the cells isolated from a human embryo could undergo before dying was about fifty. When cells were taken from an older person, they divided even fewer times before dying. Cells taken from adults, for example, could divide only about twenty times.

Hayflick and other researchers also cultured cells from animals, and showed that the number of times those cells could divide depended on how long the animal normally lived. Cells from a mink, for example, which has a life span of about ten years, could not divide as many times as those of a human; and cells from a mouse, which has a life span of about three years, could not divide as many times as those of a mink. Hayflick concluded that the death of all such cells, animal and human, was an expression of aging at the single-cell level, and that the reason the cells aged was that they had a built-in genetic limit to their life spans.

This genetic limit, Hayflick thinks, is dictated by information carried in the long, complex chains of atoms of DNA in the nucleus of each cell. Aging is thus a built-in part of our cellular structure; all normal cells are predestined to undergo irreversible decline.

These conclusions were not welcomed by the scientific community, much of which remained staunchly true to the conventional wisdom that cells grown in culture had to be immortal. Indeed, as late as 1974, Hayflick stated that, "Even today, thirteen years after the initial research has been confirmed in literally hundreds of labs around the world, many still refuse to accept the findings."

Support for Hayflick's genetic-limit theory of aging comes from studies of identical twins, such as those performed by Dr. Lissy Jarvik of Columbia University. Identical twins, unlike other people, both have the same DNA in all their cells. This is because, in the case of such twins (not fraternal twins), when the fertilized egg first divides in the mother's uterus, instead of forming two cells that are part of one embryo, it forms two single-celled embryos, identical with one another in all aspects, including DNA. These twins are therefore identical not only in all those body characteristics controlled by DNA—hair color, eye color, height, facial features, and so on—but also in all the chemical processes (also controlled by DNA) going on inside each of their cells. If the DNA in the cells of identical twins has information which results in a built-in limit to the life span of each individual, then both twins should have similar life spans. And Jarvik's studies indeed show that the life spans of identical twins are generally the same.

Hayflick calculated, on the basis of fifty divisions by cultured embryonic human cells, that man's life span should be about 110 to 120 years, since that is how long it would take for that many cell divisions to occur in the body. But only about one-tenth of 1 percent of all humans ever live to the advanced age of 110. This fact puzzled Hayflick, because if human body cells could live in culture the equivalent of 110 to 120 years, then in theory the bodies those cells came from should also live that long.

When Hayflick examined the cell cultures more closely, he

found that, long before they ceased to divide, they showed specific changes in their structure and functioning—changes such as less ability to produce enough energy, less ability to make enzymes quickly enough, and more waste materials inside each cell. Thus, Hayflick concluded, these age changes in cells "play the central role in the expression of aging in the body and result in the death of the individual . . . well before its cells fail to divide." When a complex, interdependent collection of cells such as the human body has accumulated enough aging damage in its vital organ cells—such as those in the heart or brain—the whole body dies, even though there may be many cells still capable of living. This implies that if we could slow down the structural and functional changes occurring in our cells, then we might be able to live as long as Hayflick's "genetic limit."

A number of theories have been proposed to explain how Hayflick's genetic limit is expressed in the cells of our bodies. All assume that aging represents a loss of control over various bodily processes, and many assume that the control loss occurs at the cellular level in the DNA of those cells. The five major current aging theories are:

1. the error hypothesis;
2. the free radical theory;
3. the crosslinkage theory;
4. the brain hypothesis; and
5. the autoimmune theory.

Although most gerontologists agree that there is probably no single cause of aging, the proponents of each theory have accumulated evidence for their ideas on aging—and, more importantly, have produced experimental results that, according to Alex Comfort, "look most rewarding at the moment, from the viewpoint of understanding and modifying age processes."

OF MICE AND MEN

Most of the experiments, as you will see, have been performed on rats and mice and have proven that it is possible to alter the course of aging in these animals. But are the results of any use in preventing aging in humans?

There are several answers, perhaps the most convincing being that gerontologists would not bother doing animal research if they did not think it might somehow be of benefit to people. The goal of gerontologists is not to extend the life span of rats and mice; it is to extend the healthy lives of people.

From a biological viewpoint, there are compelling reasons for believing the research results from rodents will be applicable to humans. Rats and mice are mammals—fur or hair-covered animals that nurse their young—and we are too. All mammals, including humans, are subject to many of the same diseases, need much the same diets to remain healthy, have the same organs and hormones, and generally show the same course of aging, although the stages that take years in humans may only take months in rats and mice. In fact, this is one reason why these small animals are useful for experiments; since they live only about three years, the outcome of an experiment on extending life can be resolved within a short time.

In addition, on the cellular level, where much of aging may actually occur, humans are essentially identical to rodents. Both human and rodent cells are controlled by DNA, which expresses itself by making RNA, which in turn causes proteins to be made. If, as many gerontologists believe, the cause of aging lies in cells, then any factor that affects the processes of aging in rodent cells, by affecting rodent DNA, RNA, or protein, has a high probability of affecting the same processes in human cells in the same way.

Many of the advances in modern medicine that, since the beginning of this century, have extended all our lives by about thirty years were made possible by work on rodents and lower organisms. Life-saving drugs such as penicillin were first tested in rodents. This procedure of testing animals before humans has become so accepted that federal law now *requires* that all drugs be tested on animals before they are tested on humans.

There are, of course, differences between rodents and humans, and some things that might prove effective in lengthening the lives of rodents might not prove effective in humans. But as Alex Comfort states, "It is extremely likely that the known techniques of rodent life-span modification would produce some effects on human aging rates if they could be quickly and ethically tested."

THEORY NO. 1: AGING BY MISTAKE

The chemical reactions of metabolism occurring inside cells do not happen with 100 percent accuracy. Cells can make "mistakes" in producing new DNA, RNA, or proteins because the metabolic machinery is not 100 percent accurate. Polluting chemicals—exhaust fumes, factory smoke, cigarette smoke—in the air, food, and fluids we take in can also attack the DNA, RNA, and protein molecules. Thus, our bodies have sensitive repair mechanisms consisting of a number of different enzymes that can recognize such defective and damaged molecules and either destroy them or repair them. But even these repair systems are imperfect, and relatively subtle errors can escape detection.

Many gerontologists feel that aging is the result of these accumulated unrepaired errors. As Hayflick says, "the loss of accurate or reliable [control] information is seen to occur from accumulation of random events which damage the essential . . . molecules of DNA, RNA, and protein. When a threshold of 'hits,' 'damage,' 'insults,' or 'errors' is reached, normal biological activities cease and the manifestation of age-related changes then become evident. The precise nature of damage to such essential molecules is not known, but the fact of their occurrence is known."

Some gerontologists, such as F. Marott Sinex of Boston University School of Medicine, think that it is errors in DNA which are the key to aging. Permanent changes in the chemical structure of the long chains of atoms that make up DNA are called mutations. According to Sinex, mutations represent a change in the information, carried by DNA, which controls cellular functions. Mutations can result from unrepaired errors in the production of new DNA, from errors in the repair process, or from attacks on DNA by polluting chemicals. A mutation in the DNA of a cell can lead that cell to produce an altered RNA, which in turn results in the cell making an altered protein enzyme. The altered enzyme may not function as well as the normal enzyme, or it may not function at all.

The metabolic reactions governed by that defective enzyme will then cease, and the cell will no longer perform well or may even die.

This theory of aging by the accumulation of mutations was first proposed in 1954 by the physicist Leo Szilard, who came to his conclusion by observing the life-shortening effect of radiation on animals and humans. Radiation causes many mutations in DNA, and it also hastens the appearance of certain signs of aging, such as greying hair and cancer. Szilard reasoned, therefore, that mutations in animals and humans were the cause of aging. Although he could not explain how such mutations arose in animals and humans *not* exposed to radiation, he felt that it was probably the result of natural damage to cells.

Today, some gerontologists such as Dr. Howard J. Curtis, of Brookhaven National Laboratory in New York, feel that Szilard is correct in his assumption that aging is due to the slow accumulation throughout life of unrepaired mutations that destroy the functional capacities of the cells. And Curtis also feels that aging due to mutations may be prevented, or at least slowed down, by augmenting, through genetic engineering, the processes in body cells responsible for DNA repair.

Some researchers think that aging due to DNA mutations is not as significant as that due to unrepaired damage to RNA, proteins, and enzymes. Dr. Leslie Orgel, of the Salk Institute in La Jolla, California, has suggested that mistakes in RNA and protein production can cause aging in cells through what he terms "error catastrophes." Each RNA molecule produced by DNA is responsible for the manufacture of many copies of a particular protein enzyme; the RNA serves as a "mold" from which a number of identical copies of a protein are made. Thus, if the RNA is defective, then each of the protein molecules produced from it will be defective, and will not function efficiently in driving chemical reactions in metabolism. In addition, certain enzymes assist in the production of proteins made from RNA molds, while others assist in the production of RNA from DNA. Once an error is made in RNA or protein, then, it will continue to result in more faulty "molds," leading to a cumulative increase of errors until the last "error catastrophe" occurs—death.

Researchers have found that enzymes from aged cultured human cells are abnormal in function—that in fact as much as 25 percent of some enzymes are defective—showing that Orgel's "error catastrophe" theory may be correct. The evidence is still not conclusive, but there is reason to hope that attempts to modify the course of error-induced aging may be successful. It may not be necessary to treat the primary molecular error but rather its consequences. One way to slow down the accumulation of errors, Alex Comfort suggests, might be to slightly lower the metabolic rate of body cells, reducing the probability that an error will occur. This could be done by lowering body temperature, which has been shown to extend the life spans of lower animals, such as fish and turtles. By using techniques now being developed, such as those described in the previous chapter, we may be able to do the same.

THEORY NO. 2: THE RAVAGES OF FREE RADICALS

Pictures or models of DNA, RNA, and protein molecules often depict them as rigid, static structures like bridges, but they are actually unstable, long, chainlike structures composed of thousands of molecules that can easily fall apart. In the cell environment they are constantly subject to attack by other molecules, some of them normal products of metabolism, others environmental pollutants such as lead. New molecules are therefore being made all the time in cells to replace the ones that are damaged.

During the course of metabolism, certain molecules are produced, called free radicals, which have a strong tendency to link to other molecules. Cells sometimes produce free radicals to assist in metabolism, most commonly during those reactions involving the use of oxygen to "burn" sugar to produce energy. Sometimes, free radicals can be produced by accident if oxygen, always present in the cell and highly reactive, combines with the cellular molecules.

Alex Comfort has compared a free radical to "a convention delegate away from his wife; it's a highly reactive chemical agent that will combine with anything that's around." The result is that uncontrolled free radicals can cause accumulated damage to the membranes surrounding cells and to the cellular molecules of RNA and DNA. This would make it a major determinant of biological aging.

One attack on free-radical aging is the use of chemicals called antioxidants. Interestingly, one of the most active research programs on antioxidants has been conducted by the food packaging industry, which is looking for ways to counteract damage caused by free radicals to stored food that is exposed to oxygen in the air. The commonest antioxidant is called BHT, and is produced by the food industry in huge amounts each year. If we look at the labels on cereal, gum, margarine, soda, potato chips, and other foods, they often state, "BHT added to preserve freshness." Studies by Dr. Denham Harman of the University of Nebraska College of Medicine—a former Shell Oil chemist who became so fascinated by Alexis Carrel's "immortal" chicken cells that he quit to go to medical school in order to become a researcher into aging—has shown that rats fed BHT live up to 20 percent longer than rats not given BHT. Following Harman's lead, Comfort showed that another antioxidant, ethoxyquin, could increase the life span of mice by about 25 percent. Other antioxidants appear to prolong the life of rats or mice 15 to 20 percent.

BHT and other antioxidants at present are not considered safe for human consumption in the enormous amounts proportional to those used in animal experiments. Still they point the way to a possible method for life extension, through the development of safer antioxidants.

Another attack on free radical aging was demonstrated in 1973 by Dr. Richard Hochschild, president of Microwave Instruments Co. in Corona Del Mar, California. Injecting mice with a drug called Centrophenoxine, Hochschild found it increased their lives by about 40 percent. Hochschild also gave the drug to aged mice and found that it increased their remaining life span by 11 percent.

Centrophenoxine is a drug in use in Europe and elsewhere, but not in the United States, for relieving the symptoms of a number of disorders originating in the brain, such as reading problems, speech difficulties, and impaired muscular control. According to Hochschild, it does not seem to be toxic to the test animals and it has a definite life-prolonging effect. In addition, it has been used for some time to treat humans with brain disorders and therefore seems safe in humans as well as rats. Only further research will show if Centrophenoxine can be effective in lengthening our lives, but it should be

noted that the drug is derived from the chemical dimethylamino-
ethanol, which is related to another chemical (diethylaminoethanol)
that is produced when the antiaging drug Gerovital is injected into
humans.

Still another possible approach to slowing free radical aging is
varying the diet. Nebraska's Dr. Harman points out that fats, especially the polyunsaturated kind found in oils and other plant-derived
foods, have been proven to participate in free radical reactions and
therefore might increase the rate of aging. By feeding mice increased
amounts of polyunsaturated fats, or increasing the proportion of
such fats in their diets, Harman has decreased their life spans.

Vitamin E also confers protection from free radical damage.
"Aging is due to the process of oxidation," says Dr. A. L. Tappel of
the University of California at Davis, "and since Vitamin E is a
natural antioxidant, it could be used to counteract this process in
the body." Although Tappel has so far been unable to demonstrate
that additional Vitamin E can prolong the lives of rats or mice, he
has shown that inadequate amounts of the vitamin in their diets will
definitely shorten their lives. He has also examined the diets of
Americans and has found they are inadequate in a number of ways,
including insufficient Vitamin E. "Because the biochemistry of Vitamin E deficiency and the aging processes . . . run parallel," he says,
"it is apparent that there should be concern about the low Vitamin
E levels in human beings . . . optimization of Vitamin E intake may
slow those aging processes."

Tappel also points out that the diet must also include adequate
amounts of Vitamin C because it acts synergetically, enabling Vitamin E to defuse free radicals more efficiently. By making various
adjustments in our diets, such as lowering the amount of polyunsaturated fat from about 20 percent of our calorie intake to about 1
percent, and getting enough Vitamins C and E, Harman says, "it
might be possible by acceptable, practical dietary means to increase
the life span." Indeed, he feels, applying this approach to persons in
the latter part of the life span might have a significant beneficial
effect. Such "free radical diets," Harman concludes, offer "the
prospect of an increase in the life span to beyond eighty-five years as
well as the possibility that a significant number of people will live to
be well beyond 100 years."

THEORY NO. 3: CROSSLINKAGE-CAUSED AGING

Dr. Johan Bjorksten heads the Bjorksten Research Foundation in Madison, Wisconsin, a nonprofit organization he founded in 1952 to conduct gerontological research. Bjorksten got his start in gerontology in a rather odd fashion. In the early 1940s he was a biochemist for Ditto, Inc., at that time the world's largest manufacturer

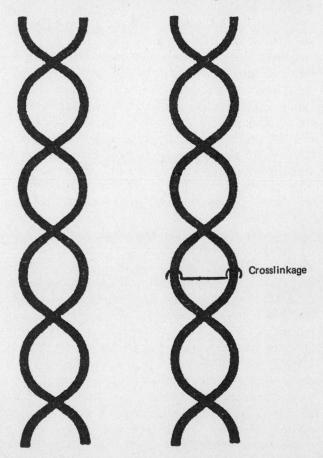

Crosslinkage

Crosslinkage. Normal DNA (left) is compared with crosslinked DNA.

of the films used in pre-Xerox copying processes, doing research in trying to prevent the film from breaking down ("aging") and losing its ability to make copies. The main constituent of the film, besides the added chemicals that produce the copy, is gelatin, a semisolid solution of proteins in water. Bjorksten noticed that the aging processes in the film's gelatin and in similar protein structures in the body—such as in cartilege and tendons—were alike. Both processes involve protein reactions leading to loss of elasticity.

What struck Bjorksten was that the stiffness in the muscles and joints of older people bore a close similarity to the process of "tanning" whereby proteins, such as those in leather or gelatin, are hardened through the application of various chemicals. Bjorksten knew that tanning resulted from the formation of chemical "bridges" between the proteins, called crosslinkages, and felt that human aging might be due to a similar formation of crosslinkages. In 1942 he expressed his ideas on aging by crosslinking, saying, "The aging of living organisms, I believe, is due to the occasional formation, by ... crosslinkage, of bridges between protein molecules, which cannot be broken by the cell repair enzymes."

As Bjorksten refined his protein crosslinkage theory, he realized that there was a second possible type of crosslinkage damage. This was the formation of crosslinkages in the DNA molecules. As the illustration shows, DNA consists of two long, twisted strands of atoms loosely connected by chemical linkages. When crosslinkages form between the two strands of DNA, they cannot be undone by the cell's normal repair mechanisms, according to Bjorksten. This irremovable "bridge" between the two strands interferes with the production of RNA by the DNA, in turn preventing the production of vitally needed proteins that would have been produced by that RNA. In addition, the crosslinkages prevent DNA from participating in cell division, so that cells may not be replaced.

Crosslinkages in protein and DNA can be caused by many chemicals normally present in cells as a result of metabolism and by common pollutants such as lead and tobacco smoke. When one counts up the number and amount of crosslinkage-causing chemicals in the body, Bjorksten says, the question becomes not "Is this sufficient to cause aging?", but rather "How is it possible that aging proceeds as slowly as it does?"

Evidence for Bjorksten's theory has been produced by Dr. E. Heikkinen of the University of Turku in Finland, who demonstrated an age-dependent increase in the number of crosslinkages in rat skin. Other researchers have shown similar increases of crosslinkages with age in arteries, cartilege, and muscle not only in rats but also in humans.

Bjorksten's contributions have not stopped at the theoretical. For a number of years, he has been actively pursuing research that he feels may have practical application in alleviating crosslinkage-caused aging. One line of research has been into soil bacteria that have the ability to unlink crosslinked molecules, bacteria that live in an environment where their principal food source is crosslinked molecules from dead organisms such as fallen leaves. Some of these bacteria, Bjorksten believes, make protein enzymes that allow them to dissolve these crosslinked molecules into digestable bits. So far, Bjorksten has isolated about 140 such cultures of bacteria. He succeeded in isolating enzymes from these bacteria, and found that one in particular was effective in dissolving crosslinkages in dead human tissue. In tests on live mice, he found the enzyme was not toxic; moreover the mice aged more slowly and lived slightly longer than did mice not receiving the enzyme. It is not possible, however, to form any firm conclusion from these few animal tests, which were intended only to check for toxicity.

Helping to slow down or reverse aging may not be the only potential use for Bjorksten's enzymes. An exciting possibility exists that they may be effective in dissolving the material that causes arteriosclerosis. Arteriosclerosis—"hardening of the arteries"—is the major killer of American males because it causes heart attacks and strokes. Although we still do not know a lot about arteriosclerosis, the "hardening," which consists of a combination of fats and protein in the walls of arteries, is held together by enormous amounts of crosslinkages. If Bjorksten's enzymes could be shown to relieve arteriosclerosis, it is possible they could add up to twenty years to the average person's life span by helping to prevent heart attacks and strokes.

THEORY NO. 4: BREAKDOWN OF THE BRAIN PACEMAKER

Our bodies function well only if all the parts are interacting smoothly and in the right order. This need for the integrated functioning of the parts of the body was first realized in the nineteenth century by the brilliant French philosopher and physiologist Claude Bernard. Research by Bernard contributed to our knowledge of how digestion works, how the liver functions to store sugar so that it can be used when needed, and how the brain, heart, and placenta work.

Bernard noted that the cells in the body are bathed in an extracellular fluid, a bloodlike solution responsible for transporting nutrients and oxygen from the blood to the cells and for carrying away wastes, such as carbon dioxide, from the cells to the blood. Bernard was impressed by the importance to the body of maintaining this fluid so that the cells could continue to function, and he referred to the extracellular fluid as the *milieu intérieur*—the internal environment of the body. "It is the fixity of the internal environment," he stated, "which is the condition of free and independent life ... All the vital mechanisms of the body, however varied they may be, have only one object, that of preserving constant the conditions of life in the internal environment."

Other physiologists also began to realize that all parts must operate together in order for the body to function properly. In the early part of this century, Walter Cannon, professor of physiology at Harvard University, called the ability of the body to regulate the functioning and interactions of its parts homeostasis—from two Greek words meaning "standing" and "similar." Cannon pointed out that homeostasis for the whole body was as important as Bernard had thought it was for the extracellular fluid.

The most vital elements in attaining homeostasis, according to Russian scientist V. M. Dilman, of the N. V. Petrov Research Institute of Oncology in Leningrad, Russia, are "the coordinated activity of two major regulatory systems—the endocrine and nervous systems." The endocrine glands are those organs in the body which secrete hormones into the blood—the thyroid gland, parathyroid glands, ovaries and testes, adrenal glands, pancreas, thymus, and the pituitary. Hormones are chemicals that regulate various aspects of bodily and cellular metabolism, and that also regulate, in some cases, other hormones. The endocrine glands constantly "police" the body's internal environment, monitoring for some deviation from normal, and when they encounter such deviations, they secrete their hormones into the bloodstream to bring the body back to normal. The pancreas, for example, secretes insulin into the bloodstream after a meal, when sugar from digested food enters the blood, raising the amount of sugar in the blood above normal. Insulin enables the body's cells to utilize sugar for the production of energy, as well as storing any excess sugar as fat.

The pituitary gland—the "master gland" of the body—secretes many hormones that control the release of hormones by other endocrine glands. But the "master gland" is really a "slave" of the hypothalamus, which is the center of control over bodily homeostasis. The hypothalamus, which like the pituitary, is located in the brain, controls many of our basic functions—including sleep, thirst, hunger, sexual drive, the female menstrual cycle, body water and salts balance, body temperature, blood pressure, and hormone release.

Some gerontologists such as Dilman think that many of the changes that occur in body function as people age are due to a decline in the body's ability to maintain homeostasis through endocrine and brain control. Many symptoms of aging seem to be caused by a breakdown in the control of hormone production, so that either too little or too much of the hormones are produced, driving the regulation of bodily processes into a decline. Menopause, for example, is due to the loss of the hormone estrogen, which is produced by the ovaries. The result is a decline in fertility, and vaginal secretions (which can interfere with sex), and muscle tone, thinning and drying of the skin. With menopause comes an increase in the amount of cholesterol in the blood, which means postmenopausal women are as likely as men to suffer heart disease, which may be caused by cholesterol deposits cutting off blood flow to the heart.

One of the foremost researchers studying the role of homeostatic decline in aging is Dr. Caleb Finch of the Andrus Gerontology Center at the University of Southern California in Los Angeles. Finch feels that homeostatic breakdown is not due to just a malfunction of the endocrine glands themselves, but to a breakdown in the control of the hypothalamus over the pituitary, which in turn causes a breakdown of control over the endocrine glands. By way of evidence, he points out that two researchers at the National Taiwan University, Ming-Tsung Peng and Hive-Ho Huang, have shown that old ovaries from female rats that had undergone menopause that have been transplanted became "rejuvenated" to the extent that they again began to produce eggs. Moreover, in Britain researchers showed that young female rats could be fertilized even after they received old ovaries transplanted from postmenopausal, sterile females, and that the offspring were normal in every way. This may mean, Finch says, that since the ovaries and other endocrine glands are regulated by the hypothalamus, the breakdown in endocrine homeostasis does not originate in the endocrine glands but in the hypothalamus.

Other evidence that the breakdown in homeostasis which may lead to aging is centered in the hypothalamus has been produced by Dr. Joseph Meites, of Michigan State University. Meites was able to induce ovulation in aged female rats by giving them a drug called L-DOPA (for dihydroxyphenylalanine). This drug increases the amount of certain brain molecules called catecholamines, which are concentrated in the hypothalamus and other parts of the brain. Catecholamines may be the control chemicals that some cells in the hypothalamus secrete in order to control the pituitary gland—which in turn secretes hormones that control the other endocrine glands, thereby regulating almost all vital processes in the body. Thus, Finch concludes, "Changes in a limited, critical population of cells in the brain (e.g., the hypothalamus) could have many consequences throughout the body ... these cells may serve as pacemakers of hormonal aging."

Meites' experiments with L-DOPA to increase catecholamines indicates that relatively simple adjustments of body chemicals might correct hypothalamic breakdown. L-DOPA has been used for years with nearly no side effects in the treatment of persons suffering from Parkinson's disease. It may therefore prove safe to use the drug as an antiaging treatment.

Indeed, there is already evidence that L-DOPA treatment can be effective in extending life span. In 1974, George C. Cotzias of the Brookhaven National Laboratory in New York showed that L-DOPA fed to mice could "significantly extend their life span and apparent prime of life." In those experiments, twice as many mice survived to eighteen months after being fed L-DOPA as those not fed the drug. Cotzias says he has also given large doses of L-DOPA to human subjects with no harmful side effects, although the levels were still not as high as those fed to mice. He also points out that cattle have been regularly fed with the velvet bean, a plant food that can contain enormous amounts of L-DOPA, up to three times as much as that fed to the experimental mice, and no side effects have been noted. Drugs called monoamine oxidase inhibitors, used by psychiatrists to control depression in some patients, could also, some doctors feel, be used to increase the amount of catecholamines in people's brains.

THEORY NO. 5: AUTOIMMUNE AGING

The body's immune system protects it from disease and cancer. As we mentioned earlier, the major components of the immune system are two types of white blood cells, B cells and T cells. The main job of the B cells is to fight bacteria, viruses, and cancer cells by releasing proteins called antibodies, which attach themselves to the disease organisms and help tear them apart. The main job of the T cells is to attack and destroy cells foreign to the body, such as cancer cells and transplant cells.

Dr. Roy Walford of UCLA postulates that B and T cells malfunction with age, and as a result cancer increases as people get older because the B and T cells no longer vigorously attack cancer cells. Another result is that B and T cells behave abnormally, attacking not only disease organisms and cancer cells, but the body's own normal, healthy cells. This destruction of the body by its own protective immune system is called autoimmunity. "Aging is an . . . autoimmune process," Walford says, and points out that there are a number of known autoimmune diseases that produce symptoms of aging—for example, rheumatic fever, which damages the heart valves; glomerulonephritis, which destroys the kidneys; and rheumatoid arthritis, which causes progressive deterioration of the joints. "The normal process of aging in man," says a UCLA colleague of Walford,

Dr. Patricia Meredith, "may be analogous to a type of autoimmune phenomenon involving all body tissues."

Dr. William H. Adler, of the National Institute on Aging in Maryland, writing on the "intriguing hypothesis that there may be an association between the functions of the immune system and aging phenomena," says that there is evidence that antibody production declines with age in humans and so does T cell function.

There may be methods for "rejuvenating" the immune system in order to prevent the development of autoimmune aging. In 1969, Dr. Takashi Makinodian, a colleague of Adler's at the National Institute on Aging, showed that removing the spleen from aged mice almost *doubled* their life spans—as Alex Comfort says, this is "one of the largest recorded increases in life span."

The spleen (an organ that can often be removed, when injured, without any apparent consequence) lies under the left lung and next to the stomach. It serves as a reservoir for red-blood cells; in a major accident, when blood is lost, the spleen releases its stored red-blood cells into the circulation. The spleen is also a reservoir for T cells, and assures that, as the thymus ages and slowly loses its ability to produce new T cells, there will still be enough T cells in the body.

Because it is a reservoir of T cells, Makinodian reasons that the spleen probably contains, in older animals (and humans) many defective T cells that can cause autoimmune aging, and this is why removing the spleen from older animals prolongs their lives. In addition, Makinodian has shown that injecting spleen cells from older mice into younger mice shortens the latters' life spans; he concludes that the spleen accounts at least in part for senescence and death and that its removal "significantly prolongs life expectancy."

Makinodian cautions, however, that simply removing the spleen will not be totally effective in lengthening life because the spleen also contains many functional T cells needed to fight disease and cancer cells. After the spleen is removed, according to Makinodian, the individual must be given injections of functional T cells, either from his own body, stored frozen when he was young, or from another, a younger donor with matching tissues. Removing T cells from a young person is possible because the thymus and spleen quickly replace the lost T cells. Makinodian has done preliminary experiments of this type of "T cell rejuvenation" by injecting T cells from young rats into old rats. Such "rejuvenated" old rats survive disease better than untreated old rats. He concludes that if the spleen is removed before the young, functional T cells are injected into an older individual, then "Transfer of juvenile T cells might permit the T cells to considerably prolong life."

Autoimmune aging may also be slowed or reversed by the use of thymosin, a hormone produced by the thymus. This hormone was discovered in 1965 by Dr. Allan Goldstein, of the University of Texas Medical School in Galveston. Thymosin, he thinks, seems to be responsible for maintaining the function of T cells. Goldstein was also aware that there is a class of T cells, helper T cells, that assist B cells in some still unknown manner in making antibodies. Thymosin, he concluded, should therefore help maintain B cell function, as well as T cell function, by keeping "helper" T cells active. Thymosin is present in the thymus of many animals, such as mice, rabbits, and cows, as well as in humans, but Goldstein uses thymosin extracted from cows in his research, since it is also active in humans. Just as cow insulin has been used to treat diabetes in people, a procedure that has saved thousands of lives since its first use in 1921, perhaps cow thymosin may be used to treat autoimmune aging in humans.

Goldstein has shown that thymosin decreases with age in human subjects, and so, he feels, a lack of thymosin could be responsible for the increased incidence of cancer found in older people, as well as for the rise in autoimmune disease thought by Walford to be responsible for aging. There is thus strong evidence that a lack of thymosin contributes at least partially to autoimmune diseases, and even the degenerative changes of old age. Goldstein has already shown that thymosin may be effective in treating certain types of cancer. Further research will reveal whether it might be useful in slowing or reversing autoimmune aging.

Diet, too, may slow autoimmune aging—particularly restricted diets. Over four decades ago, in 1935, Clive McCay of Cornell University showed that giving rats only enough food to maintain their body weight increased their life spans up to 25 percent. Other researchers have demonstrated the life-lengthening effects of dietary restriction in older animals. For example, in 1968 D. S. Miller and P. R. Payne of Queen Elizabeth College in London found that restricting the amount of protein in the diets of older rats lengthened their lives by 28 percent.

In all these experiments the rats had less calories than in the normal diet given rats, but the diet was adequate in nutrition; it contained enough protein, sugar, fat, and vitamins to maintain health. In fact, it has been shown that older animals fed a restricted diet have less cancer, kidney disease, and heart disease than do animals fed a normal diet. Alex Comfort says the research on dietary restriction has been so successful that it "remains the most effective known method of modifying the apparent rate of ... senescence."

The life-lengthening effects of dietary restriction, according to UCLA's Walford, are due to its slowing the rate of autoimmune aging, "The great prolongation of life induced by dietary restriction," he says, "might be explained by the fact that the immune system is ... more susceptible than any other body system to starvation." Dietary restriction does not seem to harm the immune system; instead it slows its decline by slowing its activity, so that in animals at least T and B cells remain "younger" longer. In fact, Walford has shown, dietary restriction slows the activity of the immune system in young mice, but actually increases T and B cell activity in older mice, making them more resistant to disease and evincing less symptoms of autoimmune aging than old mice fed a normal diet.

Thus, restricting our diets by eating less, but maintaining adequate amounts of nutrition, may slow the rate of autoimmune aging, a possibility that Comfort feels has not received enough attention. "In view of its importance as a tool in slowing ... aging ... dietary restriction has received inadequate study by critical experiment."

When the biological basis of aging is finally revealed, undoubtedly it will also include a genetic compenent. Coupling genetics, a field of great research advances, with the knowledge gained in the study of the biology of aging, will almost certainly give mankind great life-extending benefits. The areas of most intense research are described in the next chapter.

8. Genetic Engineering

The Asilomar Conference Center, on the rugged California coast just north of Carmel and Big Sur, is surrounded by huge redwoods and pines. The buildings are made of rough stone, like an early American church, and the center itself has been the site of numerous academic conferences on a multitude of topics from civil rights to freedom of the press.

On February 24, 1975, a cold, clear day, 140 of the world's leading geneticists and molecular biologists came together to debate whether science had the right to proceed with experiments that might lead to new forms of life on earth. The conference was called by Stanford University geneticist Paul Berg, an athletic, Lasker Prize-winning scientist. It was also attended by three Nobel Laureates—James D. Watson, the rumpled, tousle-haired director of the Cold Spring Harbor Laboratory of Quantitative Biology in New York, who in 1953 discovered with Francis Crick the exact configuration of DNA; Joshua Lederberg, a muscular, balding Stanford geneticist whose work penetrated into the nature of genetic mutations; and David Baltimore, a young, bearded MIT microbiologist whose work studied the reproduction of individual genes and who was co-chairman of the conference.

In addition to the Nobel winners there were present such renowned scientists as Sydney Brenner, of the Medical Research Council of the United Kingdom; David Botstein of the Cold Spring Harbor Laboratory; Andrew Lewis of the National Institutes of Health in Bethesda, Maryland; and W. A. Englehardt of the Soviet Union; as well as lawyer Daniel Singer from the Institute of Society, Ethics, and the Life Sciences at Hastings-on-Hudson, New York; and Robert Dworkin of Indiana University. The conference was also observed by representatives from the National Institutes of Health—the largest of the government-funded research organizations—and by the press.

Berg had called the conference because of a discovery he and some colleagues had made two years earlier that enabled them to take strings of genes from one organism, a mouse, for example, and combine them with those of another organism, such as a frog. The awesome implications of this discovery were that scientists now had the potential for creating organisms that had never existed on earth before and for radically altering the traits of existing organisms. This process, called genetic engineering, could be used either for potentially good purposes, such as altering human characteristics to extend life, or for bad, such as to create virulent strains of microorganisms for use in warfare. There was in addition to these two possibilities the chance that new strains of possibly harmful test organisms being developed simply for study purposes might accidentally escape from the laboratory, creating biological havoc throughout the world and leading to countless deaths.

FROM PEA PLANTS TO DNA

The terrifying results obtained by Berg and his associates culminated over a century of research into the genetics mechanisms by which living creatures inherit the ability to carry on the life-giving chemical processes that determine their structure and function. The modern study of genetics began in the mid-1800s in the garden of the monastery of St. Thomas in Brünn, Austria (today a part of Czechoslovakia), where Gregor Mendel, who had become an Augustinian monk in order to escape the grim poverty of his boyhood, grew thousands of pea plants.

Mendel had a strong interest in science, and from 1851 to 1853, on leave from the monastery, he attended the University of Vienna, and studied physics, mathematics, and plant physiology. Excited by the new knowledge he had gained there from some of the great experimental plant breeders such as Carl Friedrich Gartner, Mendel returned to the monastery and carefully set out to investigate the nature of inherited characteristics in living things. Growing his pea plants (which he called "my children") and fertilizing them by hand, he crossed (mated) them according to height and color, then tabulated the results, applying his new knowledge of mathematics to analyze how plants inherit specific, observable characteristics.

In 1865, in two lectures before the Brünn Natural Science Society, he outlined his eight years of research. But though his audience included local scientific notables, they did not understand Mendel's mathematical explanation of the distribution of height, color, and other characteristics in the plant crosses he had performed. They also did not understand his original theoretical conception of inheritance. There were no questions and no discussion of the results. Nor were they the only ones to fail to understand the tremendous significance of what he had accomplished. Mendel published the results of his work in the Brünn *Natural Science Society Proceedings* for 1865—and for thirty-five years they were completely ignored by all other researchers who were also trying to unravel the mysteries of inheritance that Mendel had already successfully completed.

Exactly what Mendel discovered, through his pea crosses, is that the characteristics of living things, such as flower color in peas and eye color in humans, are produced as the result of the action of units within their cells. These units later were given the name genes (from the Greek word for "reproduction").

Mendel said that living things inherit genes from their parents, and once they are received, some "formative element" inside the cells of the offspring causes the genes to be expressed as a characteristic, such as seed color or hair color. The genes living things inherit from their parents, as Mendel showed, contain all the information necessary to produce the characteristics of those living things.

When Mendel died in 1884, he left behind only a few letters and one published manuscript in the journal of an obscure, provincial scientific society.

It was not until 1900 that three researchers—Carl Correns at the University of Tubingen in Germany; Erich von Tschermak-Seysenegg at the College of Agriculture and Forestry in Vienna; and Hugo de Vries at the University of Amsterdam—all simultaneously discovered the same principle of inheritance that Mendel had outlined thirty-five years before. At the same time, all three found, as Correns said, "that the Abbot Gregor Mendel . . . had, during the sixties [1860s], not only obtained the same result . . . but had also given exactly the same explanation." And so Mendel was finally given the credit for his discovery, and the science of genetics was born.

New developments followed quickly after the rediscovery of Mendel's work in 1900. Scientists knew that genes were localized in the nucleus of the cell, on structures called chromosomes ("colored bodies"), because the chromosomes were distributed to offspring in matings in exactly the same way as the mathematical analysis of Mendel had showed that genes are distributed. Mendel, however, knew nothing about chromosomes, which were not described accurately until the late 1800s, shortly before his death. The chromosomal theory of inheritance was published in 1903 by W. S. Sutton, a graduate student at Columbia University. At this time researchers all over the world believed that genes were composed of protein. They were visualized as being beads of protein strung together in long necklaces inside the nucleus of cells. By the end of the first decade of the twentieth century, geneticists thought that the problem of the chemical nature of inheritance was solved, and that only the details remained to be filled in.

In 1944, however, Oswald T. Avery and his colleagues at the Rockefeller Institute in New York found that genes were not composed of protein, but of DNA. The long chains of atoms that comprise DNA had been discovered in 1869 by the German chemist Friedrich Miescher, but had been thought to be of little importance to cells compared to proteins. Avery's experiments with pneumonia bacteria had shown that new characteristics could be transferred from one type of pneumonia bacteria to another by a process called transformation. If genes were composed of protein, then the characteristics controlled by those genes should be transferred with the transfer of proteins between bacteria. But, in fact, Avery showed that protein did not transfer them; only the DNA transfer did so. As Ernest Borek, a chemist at the City University of New York says, "Avery did not state it, but in effect he had isolated the genetic material of the cell. Thus the two independent paths of research stemming from the discovery of DNA by Miescher and the deduction of the laws of heredity by Mendel converged."

Avery was a shy, intense man who was so devoted to his research at the Rockefeller Institute that he lived across the street in order to be close to work. His devotion paid off in an important information key to scientists trying to determine how the genes caused the expression of inherited characteristics. Once the exact chemical nature of DNA was known, it was speculated, it might provide clues to all those characteristics DNA controlled in living things—not only eye color, but also life, aging, and death.

Avery's discovery of DNA as the chemical that makes up genes generated tremendous excitement, and researchers all over the world began studying DNA to try to uncover the secret of its operation. Two groups especially were in the forefront of this race—in the United States, Linus Pauling and his colleagues; in England, James D. Watson and Francis H. C. Crick.

Watson, an American with a Ph.D in biochemistry from Indiana University, and Crick, a British graduate student, combining the research of others, formulated an idea of the structure of DNA. In 1953, their article, published in the English journal *Nature,* began with the modest statement: "We wish to suggest a structure for . . . DNA. This structure has novel features which are of considerable biological interest." Their structure showed how the genes, composed of DNA, operate to produce the characteristics in a cell by producing RNA. The RNA acts as a "messenger" for the DNA, carrying instructions into the cell for the production of different kinds of protein, which make up the structure of the cell and produce its metabolism.

This outline of the function of a cell is called "the central dogma" because of its by now almost religious nature among scientists: DNA makes RNA which makes proteins which keeps cells alive.

If DNA is the key to life in a cell, it may also be the key to its death. There may be "death genes" that order the production of proteins that slowly age and kill cells. Or perhaps the function of DNA may decline as cells get older, leading to the eventual breakdown of the operation of the cell, causing the symptoms we call aging. Thus, many researchers since Watson and Crick have studied DNA in an effort to manipulate the characteristics of cells, including their aging.

The most successful DNA experimental techniques have involved bacteria and viruses, since they are simpler yet still exhibit the same chemical nature as other living things—they have DNA and they make RNA and protein. Viruses invade other living things, such as bacteria, plants, or animals, by overpowering and hijacking their cells and forcing them to make more virus; in this way they live. Studying viruses can therefore provide information about how DNA can control the production of RNA and protein, including any of the proteins that might bring on aging.

THE GENE-SPLICE EXPERIMENTS

Paul Berg was one of numerous scientists performing DNA research with bacteria. Many bacteria have circular pieces of DNA in them that are called plasmids, and in 1973 Berg began experimenting with a special plasmid labeled pSC101. Plasmids help make bacteria resistant to antibiotics, and this plasmid (from the bacteria *Eschericia coli*—abbreviated *E. coli*) helped the bacteria become resistant to the antibiotic tetracycline.

Berg first extracted some restriction enzymes from bacteria, enzymes that act as internal security police on the lookout for invading DNA, such as that contained in many viruses. When a bacterial cell is invaded by foreign DNA, the restriction enzymes quickly seek out the invader and dismantle it so that the foreign

DNA can serve as food for the attacked cell. In this way the cell is protected from the virus.

After Berg obtained a pure form of the restriction enzyme he desired, he placed them in a test tube with the plasmids. The restriction enzymes immediately attacked the circular plasmids.

The result of this attack on the DNA was a test tube full of long, stringy pieces of plasmid DNA with "sticky" ends. Actually, the "sticky" ends are selectively sticky: they will only stick to other DNA pieces that have been produced by the same restriction enzyme.

Berg decided to use this selected stickiness to add specific genes to the plasmids. The genes Berg used were those of a cancer-producing virus that causes tumors in monkeys. Berg isolated the

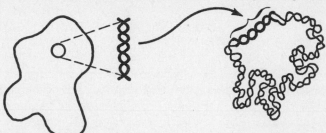

1. DNA removed from normal cell

2. Human DNA spliced to bacteria or virus DNA

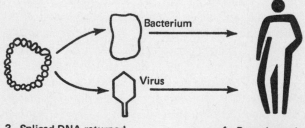

3. Spliced DNA returned to bacteria or virus

4. Bacteria or virus introduced into human

Gene splicing. How genes are spliced (1, 2). How spliced "rejuvenation" genes could possibly be introduced into humans (3, 4).

DNA of the cancer viruses and treated it with the same restriction enzyme that he had used to make the "sticky"-ended plasmids. The result was a number of cancer-virus fragments, each containing some of the virus genes and all with "sticky" ends. Berg next added these fragments to the plasmids; the "sticky" ends quickly joined, and closed, the open plasmids. Now each circular plasmid contained a fragment of the cancer virus and therefore some cancer virus genes.

These altered plasmids with their cancer-virus baggage were then allowed to invade some intact *E. coli* bacterial cells. Berg was able to show that once the plasmids were inside, their cancer-virus genes could start producing viral proteins, indicating that the viral genes had been transferred intact and functional to the bacteria. In short, Berg had by gene-splicing created a hybrid—between a cancer-producing virus and a bacterium.

The methodology, Berg states, "is simple and can probably be done as a high school science experiment."

Since then, other researchers have used plasmids to introduce frog or mouse DNA into bacterial cells. With further developments of this technique it might be possible to directly combine plants and animals into new beings not found in nature—as one Asilomar participant later jokingly put it, "to cross an orange with a duck."

But this presents tremendous hazards. To begin with, the preferred experimental bacteria, into which new genes are inserted, is the *E. coli*, a natural inhabitant of the human intestinal tract. Thus, if Berg's lab in which he combined *E. coli* bacteria with the cancer virus had allowed the new hybrid organisms to escape, the hybrid bacteria might have headed directly for the human intestinal tract. The result could have been an epidemic of human intestinal cancer.

After Berg published the results of his gene-splice experiments in 1974, he began getting requests for his restriction enzymes from researchers all over the world, who described the use to which they wished to put it. To geneticists, the ability to chop up DNA and insert it into foreign cells represented the newest tool in studying the innermost workings of cells. Geneticists hoped that with gene splicing an accurate way had been found to understand the function of individual genes.

Yet not all of the experiments with the restriction enzyme were well designed. Some that were described to Berg consisted of simply chopping up all the DNA in a cell, such as a tumor 'cell and randomly introducing the pieces into *E. coli* bacteria. This was a dangerous possibility, Berg feared, for some of the genes used by these researchers were sure to be harmful to humans and might therefore cause unforseeable damage if the *E. coli* escaped. Some experiments, it seemed to Berg, had not even been properly thought out. "I would ask people what they wanted to do with it (the restriction enzyme)," he said. "Some of them had horror experiments planned with no thought of the consequences."

In addition, Berg worried about experiments being conducted in unsafe labs. Even with the best equipment—such as sterilized, sealed labs with special ventilation and double doors with inner chambers constructed to prevent any organisms from being blown through to the outside—there have been over 5,000 accidents in the last thirty years involving dangerous organisms or toxins. Some of these accidents were harmless; others released nerve gas into the air, such as in Utah, where hundreds of sheep were killed. Still other accidents gave researchers cases of cancer, and in 1974, two researchers working in a London University laboratory and protected by over $40,000 worth of sterilization equipment were both given fatal doses of small pox while working with the virus.

One experiment that some researchers contacting Berg wanted to try was to insert into the *Staphylococci* bacteria (which cause a number of diseases in humans, including severe food poisoning, skin abcesses, infectious bone degeneration, and blood poisoning) a gene from a bacterium that is resistant to antibiotics. Testing for the effectiveness of the "gene transfusion" would be simple enough. After inserting the new genes into the staph bacteria, a colony of the hybrid staph would then be given a dose of antibiotics. If the antibiotics didn't affect the new hybrid, the experiment would be successful. If the antibiotics killed the staph, no hybridization would have occurred. But a successful experiment would have resulted in a new strain of extremely virulent, dangerous staphylococci bacteria, capable of infecting humans, yet immune to antibiotic treatment. If these bacteria got out of the lab and infected a researcher, for example, there would be no way, short of immediately isolating him, to stop the researcher from transmitting the infection to others. One could imagine an epidemic similar to the bubonic plague that swept Europe in the 1400s, killing half the population. This nightmare thought was a guiding reason for Berg's convening of the Asilomar conference.

DEBATE AMONG THE REDWOODS

Asilomar was not convened to stop research on the transplantation of genes. Rather, it was called so that the scientists themselves, without outside intervention, could set up their own standards for safety. Yet, as in the case with any group action requiring a unified decision, it was difficult to reach a common consensus.

Almost immediately the group split into two factions. The first one, nominally headed by Nobel Laureate James Watson, suggested that it was impossible to set guidelines to determine which future experiments would be safe and which would be unsafe. Watson vehemently insisted that the risk factors could not be measured and that they represented an attack on the freedom of scientific research. "They want to put me out of business for something you can't measure," he protested. To this David Botstein responded, "I would like to make a very simple argument for guidelines in this field: I'm not omniscient. My experiments usually go wrong, then I learn from them and correct my mistakes."

Botstein belonged to the other faction, nominally led by Paul Berg, which wanted to set exact standards for experiments in hopes of preventing accidents. Knowing that future risks are hard to determine—who can really predict which of a thousand experiments might produce the deadly error?—Berg fought to classify experiments as to their possible hazards and then get agreement from the geneticists not to perform those experiments considered most hazardous.

Meeting nearly twelve hours a day for four days, the group debated regulation versus the laissez-faire approach to research. Dr. Hans Maaloe, a geneticist at the University of Copenhagen, argued that it was impossible to predict accidents, and that "to imagine that we can lay down even fairly simple general rules would be deceiving ourselves." Dr. Sambrook, of Cold Spring Harbor, went even further by saying that for hazardous materials "there is no absolute containment and all containment is inefficient."

Dr. Sydney Brenner, a conference organizer, led a discussion on possible ways of producing, for experimental purposes, bacteria that would be unable to live outside of laboratory conditions.

Guidelines were drawn up and then discarded and it appeared that the debate was not going to lead to any conclusion. Berg again told the group, as they failed to take a tough enough stand, "if our recommendations look self-serving, we will run the risk of having standards imposed. We must start high and work down. We can't say that 150 scientists spent four days at Asilomar and all of them agreed that there was a hazard—and they still couldn't come up with a single suggestion. That's telling the government to do it for us."

It was not really until the lawyers began to speak to the group that a consensus was reached. Daniel Singer, of the Institute of Society, Ethics and Life Sciences, told the group that the problem of setting guidelines was ethical and that "there is no reason to shrink from the task or feel it's demeaning." Other lawyers, such as Alexander Capron of the University of Pennsylvania and Roger Dworkin of Indiana University, made the point that from accidents "million-dollar lawsuits might ensue." The lawyers impressed upon the group that in spite of the difficulties of assessing risk, they must work out guidelines because the scientists themselves are responsible for any accidents that might occur. As Dworkin said, "there is a history of disaster for expert groups who don't use the option of self-regulation." With the threat that individual researchers could be held legally and personally responsible for any damage resulting from accidents, the group finally began to work earnestly to set guidelines.

Ultimately, with the echoes of potential million-dollar lawsuits reverberating in the Asilomar air, they finally decided to divide experiments into four classes of risk: minimal, low, moderate, and high. The geneticists set guidelines for how experiments in each category were to be performed and urged curtailment of certain high-risk experiments that might produce dangerous hybrids. They also urged, as Brenner had, that new strains of bacteria be developed for experimental purposes that would be unable to live outside a laboratory environment. In their published statement, they also urged extreme caution in doing any gene-splicing experiments.

Since Asilomar, other conferences have been held under the auspices of the National Institutes of Health, the prime funder of genetics research projects. In a December 1975 meeting at La Jolla, California, NIH approved gene-splicing experiments only under certain specific conditions. The conditions included the use, for high-risk experiments, of special strains of *E. coli* (designated EK2 and EK3) that are a million times less likely to survive outside of a laboratory than ordinary *E. coli* (EK1). As Dr. Roy Curtiss III, a microbiologist at the University of Alabama, one of those developing EK2, has said, "To be cautious now is to be prudent." Progress has been fast since then, and there are already several promising EK2 strains that seem to fulfill the criteria for safety in high-risk gene-splicing experiments.

On June 23, 1976, NIH issued a set of guidelines intended to regulate all such genetic research and, in accordance with the National Environmental Protection Act, is studying the possible impact of such research on the environment. The guidelines list six categories of DNA research considered too dangerous to handle even with the best possible containment. Yet the only penalty for violating these regulations is withdrawal of NIH funding, and the guidelines say nothing about designing facilities to withstand natural disasters or precautions to take to prevent hybrid bacteria from being stolen by criminals or madmen. Indeed, there has been so much concern about the guidelines' real value that the Cambridge, Massachusetts, city council called upon Harvard to postpone further experimentation in this area, for fear of some disaster which might affect Cambridge residents. The genie that has emerged from the bottle, in other words, so far has not been capped.

GENETIC MAPPING

Biophysicist Robert Sinsheimer, a pioneer researcher in viral genetics at California Institute of Technology in Pasadena, has painted an optimistic picture about our growing mastery over genetics:

> How will you choose to intervene in the ancient designs of nature for man? Would you like to control the sex of your offspring? It will be as you wish. Would you like your son to be six feet tall—seven feet? Eight feet? What troubles you?—allergy, obesity, arthritic pain? These will be easily handled. For cancer, diabetes, phenylketonuria (a metabolic disease) there will be genetic therapy. The appropriate DNA will be provided in the appropriate dose. Viral and microbial disease will be easily met. Even the timeless patterns of growth and maturity and aging will be subject to our design. We know of no intrinsic limits to the life span. How long would you like to live? . . . Do these projections sound like LSD fantasies or the view in a distorted mirror? None transcends the potential of what we now know.

If, as Leonard Hayflick believes, aging is a result of the regulatory function of certain specific genes, then it may ultimately be possible to short-circuit those specific genes that result in decline. If aging is the result of genetic breakdown, it may also be ultimately possible to transplant new genes into humans that would repair the breakdown and enable older people to regain the level of vitality they had during youth. Genetic diseases, such as hemophilia and sickle cell anemia, also eventually may be cured by the addition of specific genes into babies after they are born. The potential for changing life will be limited by little more than the geneticists' imagination.

But in order to begin curing diseases and lengthening life with genetic therapy, we must first learn the location and function of each of the estimated 30,000 genes spaced along the DNA double helix inside the center of every human cell. To do this we must map where, along each chromosome, each gene is located. The map, once completed, will provide geneticists with a catalogue of genes which can be used in genetic engineering—to cure genetic defects and to alter the course of aging.

It was not until 1970 that it became possible for geneticists accurately to tell the difference between individual chromosomes inside human cells. Earlier the only way to tell human chromosomes apart was by size—and this was a very hit-and-miss method of determination, since chromosome size often varied greatly between specimens. But, in 1970, Torbjörn Caspersson of the University of Stockholm, experimented with a chemical dye that had the effect of "banding" the chromosomes, so that when they were viewed under ultraviolet light the individual variations on each chromosome showed up as easily recognizable bands. By 1971 the Paris Conference on Chromosome Identification had been called, and the dyes and chromosome cataloguing methods were standardized. Having a method of chromosome identification that could be used on any plant, animal, or human brought scientists nearer the successful mapping of the individual genes contained within the chromosomal body.

Caspersson's banding technique was coupled to another technique developed by G. Barski at the Institute Gustave Roussy in Paris, and the result has enabled researchers to map individual genes. Barski had found in the early 1960s that it was possible to fuse two cells together into a hybrid cell—for example, a human cell could be combined with a mouse cell to produce a human-mouse hybrid that could live and reproduce. Of course, these cells cannot produce entire animals, but they can be made to survive in the artificial culture medium in the laboratory.

This phenomenon of cell hybridization was of little practical interest until 1971. At that time Mary Weiss and Howard Green, at the Centre de Génétique Moléculaire in Gifsur-Yvette, France, hybridized mouse and human cells and allowed the hybrids to reproduce for several generations until they lost nearly all the human chromosomes (in mouse-human cell hybrids, it is the human chromosomes that are usually lost). Then by growing the hybrid cells on a culture medium that mouse cells alone would not normally grow on, they were able to determine that some of the hybrids were producing a new gene product, because they could grow on that special medium. This meant, they theorized, that the new gene product (protein) must have been created by the human chromosomes in the hybrids. Using Caspersson's newly available dye technique, they stained the hybrid chromosomes with the banding dye. Under ultraviolet light the bands showed up clearly, and the single remaining human chromosome was identified as the specific source of the gene product it commanded the hybrid cell to build.

Weiss and Green's mapping of the first single gene on a human chromosome, using the banding technique, occurred in 1971, and by 1973 the locations of twenty-eight other genes, and their functions, had also been identified. By mid-1976, 200 genes had been mapped, and Dr. Frank Raddle of Yale University, one of the leaders of the mapping research, says that new genes are being mapped at the rate of three a month. About the future of mapping, Paul Moody of the University of Vermont speculated, "It is undoubtedly only a question of time until every chromosome will be known to contain the gene for some specific enzyme. And the number of genes known per chromosome will increase [at the same time]."

GENE TRANSPLANTS

In order to use the results of gene mapping in genetic engineering, it is necessary to devise a way to inject new genes into malfunctioning cells. Successful "gene transplants" have already been accomplished both in the early hybrid experiments of the 1960s, where two dissimilar cells were fused together, and in the more sophisticated work of Paul Berg's gene splicing of restriction enzymes and plasmids. There has even been one case of gene transplantation in humans.

In 1970 two young girls, ages two and seven, were brought to the attention of Stanfield Rogers, a medical geneticist at the Oak Ridge National Laboratory in Tennessee, through a report by their pediatrician that outlined their condition as rare cases of the disease Argininemia. Argininemia is an inherited lack of the genetic ability to create a certain enzyme called arginase because of a DNA defect. Without arginase the body cannot break down accumulated amino acid waste products resulting from normal metabolism. The disease progresses slowly, as the concentrations of the waste products build up. The result is gradual damage to the kidneys and the brain as well as other tissues.

Rogers, who had been working with viruses for years, knew that if a suitable virus were found that was harmless to humans but had the ability to cause the cells it invades to produce arginase, then an injection of this virus might enable the two girls' cells to produce arginase on their own. And, in fact, for some time Rogers had known of a virus that seemed to fit these conditions. Called Shope papilloma (after Dr. Richard Shope of New York's Rockefeller Institute, who discovered the virus in the 1930s) the virus consists of a group of genes wrapped in a tight, protective protein sheath only about one-thousandth the size of a human cell. In the early 1960s Rogers had discovered that about half the scientists who were using Shope virus in their research had high arginase levels, owing to the accidental invasion of their cells by the virus.

Rogers arranged to have the girls injected with the Shope virus, and their blood chemistry was closely monitored for signs of arginase. For several months there was no change. The slow buildup of toxic amino acids continued. Cells, as a result, continued to die. But then, after months of waiting, both girls began to produce arginase. Unfortunately, the Shope virus treatment did not prove permanent. The damage to the girls' bodies from the accumulations of waste proved too great to be undone by the insertion of foreign genes, but the viability of the procedure was demonstrated.

Still, while no other humans have been medically treated by "gene transplants," a number of other researchers besides Rogers have made great strides in perfecting the techniques that will one day perhaps allow such transplants to be used. Carl Merril, Mark Grier, and John Petriccione, three researchers at the National Institutes of Health, in Bethesda, Maryland, have experimented with using viruses to carry DNA into cultured cells taken from people suffering from galactosemia. This disease is a genetic inability to produce galactose, the enzyme needed for the digestion of the sugar found in milk and milk products. In the past, people with galactosemia were treated by restricting their intake of milk and milk products, yet they often still suffered from liver disease and cataracts resulting from the buildup of galactose in their bodies.

With the viruses in effect being used as miniature hypodermic needles, genes taken from bacteria with the ability to use galactose were injected into the cultured cells taken from humans with galactosemia. Then, when galactose was added to the medium, the cells, instead of dying from galactose buildup, thrived—and were even able to pass on the ability to make the galactose enzyme to their descendants. This first demonstration, the three researchers say, is "a step toward curing diseases caused by genetic faults." Other researchers are carrying out similar research, and gene transplants may ultimately prove to be an effective treatment for the more than 2,000 genetic diseases that affect humans.

Once perfected, the genetic transplant technique may also be used to overcome many of the changes aging causes in each individual's cellular performance. If there exist certain "death genes" which key on the degeneration process in cells, then it may be possible to introduce new genes, produced synthetically or from young humans, animals, or bacteria, that will turn off the death genes. Or if aging proves to be the result of the malfunctioning of certain genes (rather than the active intervention of death genes), gene insertion may make it possible to replace or repair these poorly functioning genes. Gene transplants might even enable scientists to inject developing fetuses with new genetic information that would cancel out the death genes at birth or prevent the breakdown of genes with time.

The prospects are exciting, but, as geneticist R. Rodney Howell of the University of Texas states, "Progress in treating genetic disease can be expected to continue but at a measured pace. The problems will almost certainly have to be solved disease by disease; the likelihood of any dramatic overall 'breakthrough' seems to me very remote."

KHORANA, NIRENBERG, AND SYNTHETIC GENES

If it becomes possible to transplant genes into people, it may also become possible to insert synthetiç genes to correct genetic diseases and aging. Synthetically produced genes, once strictly in the realm of science fiction, have already been made. The first such gene was created by Har Gobind Khorana, an Indian-born American geneticist working at the University of Wisconsin and MIT. For this discovery, Khorana, at the age of forty-six, shared the 1968 Nobel Prize with Marshall W. Nirenberg of the National Heart Institute at

Bethesda, Maryland. The breakthrough that produced a clear picture of how proteins are created within a cell, and that eventually led to Khorana's synthesis of a gene, came in 1961 from Nirenberg.

What he was trying to do was to discover the "code" within the RNA that commanded each amino acid to arrange itself in the correct place in the protein. By using a simple RNA, rather than a complex natural one, he thought that he could break the code, just as a cryptographer will try to break a code by first finding the symbol that stands for "e" (the commonest letter in English) rather than trying to attack the whole code at once. Nirenberg's deduction proved correct, and the simple RNA allowed him to break part of the code—to determine exactly how the RNA commanded the amino acids in the formation of protein. Immediately Nirenberg, only thirty-seven at the time, became an international scientific celebrity. He was invited to speak before a large group of geneticists at Lomonosov University in Moscow where, said a participant, the new finding was perceived as being "nothing less than sensational: The first letter of the genetic alphabet was deciphered; the code was cracked."

In 1964, utilizing Nirenberg's discovery, Khorana set out to manufacture a completely artificial RNA. He assembled the synthetic RNA's from commercially available chemicals, and for months worked at laboriously building the chains of synthetic RNA molecules, chemical by chemical, until he finally succeeded.

Khorana's work, in creating synthetic RNA, coupled with Nirenberg's discovery of the genetic code, advanced the field of genetics tremendously. Knowing how RNA commands amino acids to form proteins greatly helped researchers learn how cell metabolism works—and how it may break down. Learning about RNA function also greatly enhanced their knowledge of how genetic information contained in the cell is expressed as life-sustaining chemical processes.

When Khorana and Nirenberg were awarded the 1968 Nobel Prize in Physiology and Medicine, each man reacted to the honor differently. Nirenberg, described as being a true genius—preoccupied to the extent of walking into objects and even tripping over his own feet—did not like the publicity. About the time he received the prize he began to have doubts as to whether it was ethical for man to tamper with genetics, and eventually decided to discontinue this line of genetic research and switched his interest to the study of behavior. Khorana was standing on a bluff overlooking the Atlantic and watching the sunset when he learned of winning the Nobel Prize. As reporters approached him, Khorana greeted them in somewhat of a daze. When asked about his reaction to the award, he replied, "I find it difficult to think. I work all the time, but then I guess we all do."

Khorana continued to work hard, and starting in 1965 and proceeding in the same precise, painstaking way as when he assembled the chemicals of RNA, he began to build a piece of DNA—to create an actual gene.

But chemically DNA is a much more complex molecule than RNA, although both are composed of essentially the same components. The DNA molecule is larger than the RNA molecule because DNA is composed of two long, twisted strands of atoms, while RNA is only a single long strand. It took Khorana five years before he was able to assemble DNA's component chemicals into a working gene. In 1970, he announced the world's first successful synthesis of a gene. The gene consisted of 154 individual parts with no part bigger than a billionth of an inch.

Other groups, such as that headed by Fotis Kafatos at Harvard University, have also successfully created synthetic genes. New, simpler techniques developed by Nobel Prize winners David Baltimore and Howard Temin have simplified the gene creation process. The Baltimore-Temin technique can be compared to using a photographic print (RNA) to make a negative (DNA). With their method, which is already being used by many research teams to mass-produce DNA, easily obtained RNA can economically be turned into gene-manufacturing assembly lines. This gene-building technique, says Jane Brody in the *New York Times,* may be useful "when science is ready to manufacture genes to perform certain desired functions, such as to supply a missing protein or neutralize the effects of an unwanted one." The "gene makers" have taken us closer to the time when we will be easily able to manufacture the genes we need to counteract aging.

In August 1976 Khorana and his associates at MIT advanced genetics one step further when they succeeded in not only artifi-

cially creating an *E. coli* gene but in actually transplanting it in a
living cell, where it worked like its real-life model. As one geneticist
said, "It was a very significant breakthrough when they synthesized
the gene. Now to have this gene working is really tremendously
exciting." Eventually, genetic diseases may be treated by substi-
tuting healthy, man-made genes for defective ones.

TURNING GENES ON AND OFF

Much of what happens as a person develops through life is the
result of turning some genes on and turning other genes off. Puberty
occurs when many genes, present since birth yet dormant, are
switched into action. Menopause occurs when genes operating in
women since age eleven or so are slowly turned off. The degeneration that accompanies aging may also result from the turning off of
genes. One way to change this on-off situation may be the intro-
duction of specific synthetic on-switches into the older body that
will command genes to produce the kind of body state they did
when the individual was younger.

Geneticists have long known that every cell contains, within its
nucleus, the entire complement of genetic information needed by
the organism. For example, a human liver cell contains not only the
genetic instructions to make a healthy liver cell but to make heart
cells, nerve cells, eye cells, and other specialized cells. Within the
DNA of each specialized cell rest thousands of dormant genetic
instructions, etched in the specific ordering of the many millions of
components that make up the genes.

But, to function properly, a liver cell (or any other cell) can
express only a certain component of its total genetic information—
the rest of the information is simply switched off. In addition, at
different times, depending upon the needs of the organism, other
genes are switched off—or on. After a person eats a sugar-rich candy
bar, for example, the body must step up its production of pancreatic
hormones which will turn some of the sugar into energy and store
some of the sugar as fat. The genes that control this pancreas
function must instruct the pancreatic cells to produce hormones
only when needed. At all other times, the genes are switched off.

In addition, certain deteriorations—such as the body's decreased ability to process and excrete cellular waste—that occur with the onset of aging may not be entirely the fault of the individual genes. Rather, it may be that the switching mechanism which is supposed to cue-on certain genes and specific processes to break down waste has either ceased working or has malfunctioned.

The path that led to an understanding of on-off switches was begun in 1946 by Jacques Monod and continued in the next two decades with Francois Jacob, both at the Institut Pasteur in Paris, the center of some of the most original and exciting work done in genetics.

Jacob started out to be a surgeon but was so badly wounded in Normandy in 1944 that he could no longer practice. Instead he obtained a doctorate in science from the Sorbonne and began with Monod to study the gene on-off mechanism in the cell. After years of study, they reached a breakthrough.

While working mutant strains of *E. coli,* they found nearly all bacterial genes had an on-off switch at one end. They called it the "operator." Other genes, they found, made protein that would combine with and cover the "operator" which would turn the genes off. This kind of gene they called the "regulator." The proteins it made that turn the genes off they called "repressors." Covering a gene operator with repressors is like putting a telegraph key in a locked drawer—the mechanism is fully functional but unable to send a message. For their discovery of the operator-regulator-repressor system, Jacob and Monod were awarded the 1965 Nobel Prize.

Khorana has followed up the research of Jacob and Monod in an effort to analyze and synthesize an on-off switch, and other researchers have done likewise. At the Laboratory of Molecular Biology in Cambridge, England, Dr. John B. Gurdon has focused on cellular chemicals termed "master switch" substances, which, he says, are responsible for turning genes on and off during development, and may also play a role in control of adult genes. Dr. Ann Janice Brothers at Indiana University has already completed the first steps toward isolating at least one master switch chemical.

The implications of this research are profound. By knowing the exact mechanisms that turn genes on and off, medical geneticists may be able to inject a person with a serum composed of on-off switches to restore crucial genetically controlled functions. Or they may be able to use the "master switch" chemicals to turn on deactivated genes while turning off others. In this way they may be able to prevent or reverse the genetic changes which some gerontologists feel cause aging.

CLONING: MAKING IDENTICAL TWINS

As we saw back in Chapter 4, transplants are successful only part of the time. It is difficult to find transplantable organs compatible with the recipient's system so that an immunological response against the transplant is avoided. But suppose organs could be grown to order, outside the body, from the transplant recipient's own cells? This way the new organ would be genetically identical with the recipient, and no immunological response would occur. That possibility may be offered by a genetic engineering process known as cloning, from the Greek word for "slip" or "twig," implying reproducing from cuttings.

As *Los Angeles Times* science writer George Alexander states, "Cloning is to biology what a photocopying machine is to business, a means of making large numbers of copies of a single object." Cloning is a form of genetic engineering by which a single cell, which contains all of an organism's genes, is made to divide into more cells until it completely reproduces the organism from which it was taken. If, for example, a single cell from an adult male were made to produce a clone, the clone would be an identical twin to that male, duplicating every fingerprint and birthmark and exactly the same DNA and proteins. As a result, an organ transplanted from a clone's body into the body of the original male would not be rejected.

As we noted, each cell contains all of the genes necessary to recreate the entire organism, but the majority of the genes in the cell are simply turned off. In 1969, proceeding on the assumption that each cell carries complete genetic information, Dr. John B. Gurdon, at that time at Oxford University in England, began experimenting with what would happen when genetic material from an adult frog cell was transplanted into the cell of a frog egg. If the nucleus of the adult cell had the correct genes, he reasoned, the egg cell would provide the necessary chemical apparatus to support development.

Gurdon placed a cell taken from the intestine of a South African clawed frog under a microscope, and with a micropipette—a glass needle thinner than human hair attached to a suction device—he pierced the adult cell membrane and removed the nucleus. He then removed the nucleus from a female frog egg cell and replaced it with the nucleus from the adult frog cell. His interest was in "whether or not the progressive specialization of cells during development is accompanied by the loss of genes no longer required in each cell type." For example, does an intestine cell nucleus retain the genes needed to produce other cell types, such as skin cells, liver cells, blood cells? If the genes were not lost, Gurdon reasoned, then it should be possible to produce a cloned frog by transferring a nucleus.

When the nucleus from the adult frog cell was placed inside the egg cell, almost immediately the egg cell began to divide; within days it became a tadpole and within weeks the tadpole became a frog. Gurdon produced several cloned frogs, and they lived, flourished, and even reproduced. Gurdon had shown, as he says, "that at least some of these intestinal cell nuclei possess all the genes necessary for the differentiation of all cell types." In short, he had proved cloning was really possible.

In Gurdon's first series of experiments, only 1.5 percent of the attempts at cloning developed into adult frogs. The reason for the low percentage of success was purely technical. If most did not reach full development, Gurdon said, it was not necessarily because they lacked the necessary genes. In some cases, it was because recipient eggs were unable to withstand nuclear injection with the micropipette. Indeed, though cloning is a relatively simple procedure, the trauma to the egg cells when injected with the micropipette has proved to be so great that most egg cells do not survive it.

But with humans there are added problems. Unlike frogs, people don't develop from eggs laid outside the female's body; human eggs must be incubated inside a womb, and they are even more delicate and susceptible to traumatic injury than are frog eggs. Also, simply injecting the genetic component of a human cell into a human egg cell that has had its genes removed will produce no results unless it then can be inserted into a human or artificial uterus. The reinsertion of a human egg is difficult, and there are only a few instances where a reinserted egg has gone to full term. In England, Dr. Douglas Bevis of Leeds University successfully reimplanted eggs which had been fertilized outside the body in a test tube back into the wombs of several women, with the result that the women gave birth to normal babies. For both cloning and artificial fertilization the reimplantation process would be the same, and at present the odds for successful reimplantation are not great. *New York Times* science correspondent David Rorvik points out that, "Out of thirty such attempts [only] three have been 'crowned with success.' "

Reimplantation too is difficult because the womb must be prepared at exactly the right time with certain hormones. The hormones are all available, but it is difficult to give the prospective mother exact concentrations. The chemical balance that enables a human embryo, after a few days, to connect itself to the wall of the womb is very delicate and difficult to achieve synthetically.

It is possible someday that a woman will be able to go to her physician, have an egg removed from her ovaries for injection with genetic material from another cell, and have the egg reimplanted into her womb. The woman might then be able to give birth to her exact genetic duplicate—or the genetic duplicate of someone else.

One future possible source of organs is limited cloning. If it becomes possible to synthetically produce the on-off switches that control the functioning of cells, it might be possible to clone single organs. The scenario, still science fiction at this point, could go something like this:

As a person loses the use of his organs, such as his lungs, through aging or disease, some of his genetic material is injected into a human egg. While the patient rests in a "cold sleep" state, the egg is inserted into a Silastic plastic uterus, an artificial womb. Inside the artificial uterus a computer monitors the precise hormonal concentrations so that normal attachment to the Silastic wall will occur. As the fetus develops, genetic repressors are injected into the synthetic blood that nourishes the growing organism, stopping all development except for that of the heart, kidney, liver or whatever organ was needed. The computer would continue to adjust levels of gene repressors in the artificial blood and in a relatively short time a perfect human heart would be available for transplanting into the chest cavity of the recipient.

Initially the newly cloned heart, which would be the size of a child's heart, would be used as an "assistant" to help the recipient recover his health and recover from the low-temperature storage, until it could grow strong enough to operate on its own. After several months the old heart would be removed and the new cloned heart would take over. Because the new heart would be cloned, rather than taken from a cadaver, there would be no rejection.

Another scenario for limited cloning is a much simpler type of procedure:

A patient suffering from heart disease, for example, would be put on a heart-lung machine for an extended period of time (this is not possible now because of the danger of blood damage). The diseased part of his heart would be removed so that a central core of healthy cells remained. These cells would be injected with heart cell "on" switches, which would stimulate them to regenerate a new heart.

There is already evidence that this latter type of limited cloning might someday be possible. At the Wistar Institute in Philadelphia, a private research organization, Vincent Cristofalo was able to get cultured human cells to continue reproducing long after they should have reached their "Hayflick's genetic limit" and stopped dividing. He did this by introducing hydrocortisone, a synthetic hormone, into their culture medium. Cristofalo hypothesizes that in normal cell division some of the daughter cells lose their capacity to divide, perhaps because they can no longer synthesize a protein necessary for division. Hydrocortisone, then, might induce the synthesis of the protein, thus reversing the process. If Cristofalo may have found a way to get old cells, such as heart cells, to begin dividing again by using certain chemicals to turn on their genes, it is conceivable that this method could be used as a way of limited cloning of organs. And, if that is possible, the regrowing of damaged organs might also become possible.

Biochemist-science writer Isaac Asimov believes that since cloning has been done in frogs, it "can undoubtedly be done in human beings." Certainly cloning can be done in mammals; it has already been done in rats and rabbits. Despite this possibility, the idea of cloning, both total and limited, raises staggering moral and social implications. Asimov sums up the problems of human cloning best when he says, "It won't be worth society's trouble, I assure you." Although, if it is perfected, cloning might be of economic significance for breeding animals—for example, in multiplying numbers of prize steer—human cloning raises too many problems.

From a practical point of view, a human in need of an organ will, when donating a cell to be cloned, have to wait a minimum of nine months for the cloned human egg to develop, and then probably another several years until the clone is old enough, and mature enough, to donate its organs. The moral issues involved in many ways outweigh even the practical ones. The basic issue is, is a clone any less a person for having been bred for its organs? Even in limited cloning if a heart were only partially cloned and there would not be the problem of having to kill an entire clone in order to derive its organs, the process still requires starting with a human egg. This would carry the abortion and "right to life" issue into new and even deeper waters.

THE YOUNG SCIENCE

Modern genetics, only about twenty-five years old, has already grown into an elaborate field yielding sensational results and raising dramatic possibilities for curing birth defects, slowing aging, and extending life. But it is a field of study that has power over our lives like no other field because the objects and processes it studies are the ones that allow all life to flourish—or vanish. With genetic engineering comes tremendous responsibility. Do we have a right to tamper with genes? Are we ready to use this powerful tool? Is it safe to try to solve aging with genetic engineering or is it like hunting butterflies with atomic bombs? And are we prepared to allow scientists to tamper with the human body, using the very same tools that could be used for creating a so-called "master race" or a population of slaves or soldiers?

No one yet knows exactly what will be the results of our inquiries. Geneticist Rollin D. Hotchkiss, of the Rockefeller Institute in New York, states that "Many of us feel instinctive revulsion at the hazards of meddling with finely balanced and far-reaching systems that made an individual what he is. Yet I believe it will surely be attempted. The pathway will be built from a combination of altruism, profit, and ignorance." And Bruno Pontecorvo, an eminent Italian physicist, sums up the difficult choices we face in the future in this thoughtful statement:

> We are just deluding ourselves if we think that human genetic engineering is only in the realm of science fiction and that we don't need to start thinking about it. My worry is that the advance will be extremely slow and minor to begin with; for instance, I would estimate that within four or five years it will be possible to cure, to a very minor, limited extent, by genetic engineering, certain genetic deficiencies; nobody will object to that and so we will go on to the next step and the next step, and so on. And if we don't start discussing these matters now, we shall get to the state, as we did with the atomic bomb, when nobody knows what is going on . . . There are innumerable possibilities and we have to be aware of them.

9. Should It Be Done?

In our century when a child is born, he takes the place of a great-grandparent, and as he draws out his three-score years and ten his lifetime spans three generations: child, parent, and grandparent. But someday the generation overlap will be enormous: a newborn baby might well be held in the arms of his great-great-great-great-great-grandmother.

As we have seen, the prospect of living 150 years is not a fantasy. "Control of human aging is something that's going to happen," Alex Comfort says. "Unless we are slothful or overcome by disaster, it's probably going to happen within our lifetimes." Bernard Strehler, of the Andrus Gerontology Center of the University of Southern California, seems to agree. "There is no substantial reason," he says, "other than lack of financial, institutional, and administrative support of critical research efforts in the field, which stands in the way of man's answering the major questions on . . . the aging process within the next decade."

It probably can be done and it probably will be done, for such has been the history of scientific accomplishment. There is a question, however, which must be faced now—should it be done? Will the planet and the human race really benefit from this massive intervention in the organization and ecology of human life as it has evolved over millions of years? Are we wiser than nature? What vision of man's potential is fulfilled by such an extended life span? What knowledge of man's current behavior makes 150 years desirable—for the individual or the human race as a whole?

The potential for disruption is staggering—as overwhelming as anything envisioned in the worst scenario of thermonuclear war. In a matter as important as this, mankind must consider the gloomiest possibilities, and from the perspectives of the problems of planet earth, the problems of our own society on the planet, and the problems of ourselves—and those of our children—within that society. In none of these areas can we offer solutions. The "facts" themselves are under heavy dispute, and yesterday's pessimistic futurist is often tomorrow's optimist. We know only that we don't know—and sometimes we even forget that. The purpose of this brief survey is only to point out that we stand at the very edge of a chasm and whether we pause here or leap before we have looked, we still will not know what is on the other side, or below, nor which direction mankind will soon be taking.

THE LIMITS OF PLANET EARTH

In March 1976, according to the Population Reference Bureau in Washington, D.C., the earth's population reached the 4 billion mark—twice the number of people that lived on the planet just forty-six years ago. At the present rate of population increase (1.8 percent a year), the world will *double* that—reaching 8 billion—in only thirty-four years. This rapid ticking-over of billion marks in just decades becomes especially awesome when one realizes that it took 2 to 3 million years to achieve the *first* billion people on this earth.

By now, of course, we know the reasons for this astronomical arithmetic: better public health and sanitation, better medical and surgical techniques for eliminating disease and extending life, and more people making more people as in any geometric progression.

These conditions apply at both ends of the life process, from infant mortality to old-age mortality. But the results of this inexorable progression could be disaster. We need only listen to some of our modern prophets on matters of food and energy resources in relation to runaway population growth to hear the hoofbeats of the four horsemen of the apocalypse.

One futurist, John Platt of the University of Michigan, raises the specter of what he calls *megafamines*—massive starvations in which 10 to 50 million people could perish. Another scholar, Dennis Meadows, author of *Dynamics of Growth in a Finite World*, predicts even greater catastrophe. If there are 7 billion people by the end of the century, he says, the stress on the world's food supply will become so great that worldwide famine will result, and by the year 2000 it is possible that 3 billion persons will have starved to death. This would not include additional millions who would die in food riots, wars, and other upheavals associated with the struggle for food.

Other futurists, utilizing computer projections of per capita energy consumption, known world resources, probable future discoveries, substitutions of new energy, production methods, etc., have come to the firm conclusion that at our current rate of population growth the world will run into energy shortages in the relatively near future that will cause overwhelming disruptions in society.

Well before the end of the century, the world may feel to a much greater degree than it already has the effects of population demands on its energy resources and on the despoliation of the environment. For example, to maintain the present U.S. standard of living, we will have to *quadruple* our Gross National Product—to almost $4 trillion—by the year 2000. This means that restraints against air and water pollution and other spoilers of the environment could become increasingly difficult as the demand for fuel and energy increases to meet production goals. And if we don't maintain the U.S. standard of living, what will the changes be? And if we do maintain it, what will the costs be to the rest of the world, to all of our political and ethical values? Can we truly prosper in a world of misery? Will we be permitted to? Population growth with our current life span obviously poses one of the great challenges to mankind's future. Although widespread life extension will obviously exacerbate the growth, it introduces some additional problems, too.

STRAINS ON SOCIETY

In the United States, people over sixty-five at present number 10 million. By the end of the century they will number 30 million and will constitute 25 percent of the population. Under today's societal definitions, then, *one out of four* people will be out of the work force, nonproductive, living on the twenty-first century version of Social Security and Medicare, and otherwise draining social and governmental resources. Even today, senior citizens require a total government subsidy of over $50 billion a year, and also often require financial assistance from family members as well. More importantly, over 20 percent of these people now live on incomes below the official government poverty threshold; that means 4 million over-sixty-five people *right now* do not have enough to eat or adequate housing or medical care by even the most minimal government standards.

At present, a person over sixty-five can expect, on the average, to live about fourteen more years after his retirement, many persons are retiring at sixty-two, and others as early as fifty-five. With so many persons out of productive service and severely taxing the resources of those still contributing to society, how can life extension do anything but aggravate the current problems associated with taking care of the aged?

Critics of life extension techniques have also raised the question of who is going to pay for them and who is going to benefit from them. Organ transplants are expensive. A heart transplant, for instance, requires two complete surgical teams (one to remove the heart from the cadaver, the other to replace the damaged heart of the living patient), and a cost of $50,000 would probably not be out of line for the operation.

Even assuming the availability of donors, it would probably be impossible for every candidate for a heart transplant to have the operation; there may simply not be enough surgical teams and supporting medical help to go around. For $50,000, then, this probably means only patients will be taken who serve some experimental purpose or who have the money. Many aspects of life extension will certainly not be democratic, any more than much medical care is today. But when the boon of money is not just a few extra years of life but an additional 75 or 100 years, the inequalities we accept today may well become unacceptable tomorrow. What would a man be willing to do to his fellow man for this gain?

Consider too the possibility of new social values. Some critics worry about the political character of a society dominated by old people. In general, older people tend to vote conservative, and liberals see the possibility of a shift in the political balance of power as the electorate becomes increasingly older. One can visualize new political divisions—life extenders versus naturalists, for instance. One can foresee antiaging techniques being used to extend the length and power of dictatorial regimes, to build elite-force armies, to perpetuate institutions that no longer serve useful purposes and which would in a more natural world wither away. Indeed, it is hard to think of even one human institution—political, business, family—that would not be profoundly changed by a doubling of the human life span.

THE MIND OF A 150-YEAR-OLD

Just as our planet and our social institutions will undoubtedly be affected by significant life extension, so we as individuals will certainly undergo profound changes and reevaluations of priorities. Many philosophers and psychologists have written that the fact of death—the knowledge of our impending demise—strongly influences many of our personal values and behavior. For instance, it has been theorized that a great deal of creativity and ambition of artists, inventors, rebels, and revolutionary figures is linked to an intense discomfort about the knowledge of one's own mortality. In one study by psychologist Lisl M. Goodman of New Jersey State College it was found that many creative people were motivated by a fear of incompleteness in their lives which would be brought about by their death. But what would happen to this impulse if one knew he could die only by accident, if he could look forward to a century and a half of life? To the extent that death gives meaning to life, the absence of death is bound to have impact on the individual psyche. If the promise of immortality is the keystone of religious belief, what will the new longevity mean for man's belief in God, the survival of religious institutions, and individual ethics and behavior? One thing is certain: we are uncertain of the effects extended life will have on the deepest parts of the human psyche. No one knows how a man with a 150-year or longer life span will view the world.

IN RESTRAINT OF CURIOSITY

The most direct challenge to research in life extension has been issued by biologist Robert Sinsheimer of California Institute of Technology. In a May 1976 paper, "An Inquiry Into Inquiry," he writes, "Curiosity is not necessarily the highest virtue—and science, the distillate of curiosity, may not merit *total* commitment."

Some forms of inquiry, Sinsheimer maintains, could yield less advantage than harm. Research into cheaper methods of isotope separation, for example, might only lead to cheaper, easier bombs. Research into predetermining the sex of children might lead to a major disruption in the balance provided by nature. Investigations into the aging process are also in this category. Is the goal of keeping our people as young as possible as long as possible, he asks, on balance a desirable goal? "I think," he answers, "there are limits to the extent to which we can rely upon the resilience of Nature or of social institutions to protect us from our follies and our finite vision."

For these reasons, Sinsheimer argues for a policy of restraint—but not prohibition—in such forms of scientific research. "Our thrusts of inquiry should not too far exceed our perception of their consequence. There are time constants and momenta in human affairs. We need to recognize that the great forces we now wield might drive us too swiftly toward some unseen chasm."

The objections to antiaging research raise extremely sobering questions, and it is important that we formulate a public policy toward the whole matter of aging and life extension. The scenarios for the future need not be catastrophic—if we plan. Let us consider the objections stated above.

THE UNLIMITED TECHNOLOGIES

The concern that runaway population growth will exhaust the world's food and energy resources is a very real one. Without question, humanity, long or short lived, must get to the task of extending its food supply, food distribution networks, and energy and resource capabilities. But the megafamines and fuel shortfalls are not here quite yet, and need not be if we quickly take advantage of the technological answers we already have. As philosopher-designer R. Buckminister Fuller stated, in January 1976, "It is feasible . . . to provide all humanity and all their generations to come with a higher standard of living and greater freedoms than have ever been experienced by any humans and to do so by 1985."

Consider food first. Throughout the world, millions are starving and going hungry, yet this need not be so. As Harvard nutritionist Jean Mayer states, there is an enormous maldistribution of food resources: "If you prepare a balance sheet by looking at all the food that is being produced in the world and dividing it by 4 billion [the world population], there is obviously enough food present."

Indeed, within this century we have witnessed a tremendous increase in farming and food-producing capabilities. In 1933, for instance, American agriculture yielded 22.6 bushels of corn per acre. Thirty years later, owing to the development of hybrid strains of corn, the figure had tripled, to 67.6 per acre. Some of the new high-yield wheat and rice strains have brought about the fabled "Green Revolution" in many parts of the world. One high-yield, high-protein strain, called Triticale, shows such great promise that Mayer declares it "the most significant development in food grain since the discovery of corn in America over 400 years ago."

North America has become the largest producer and exporter of food in the world principally because of its reliance on sophisticated machinery, fertilizers, and pesticides. However, most of these depend on oil (4 percent of the U.S. oil consumption is farm related), which, because of its cost and because it is a finite resource, might not be appropriate for other countries. Still, the use of labor-intensive simple devices—devices of intermediate technology, such as metal plows substituted for wooden ones—could significantly raise productivity in underdeveloped areas. Inexpensive new methods are also available for converting garbage into high-quality fertilizers, and other techniques for soil enrichment, some based on genetic engineering, seem to offer truly spectacular prospects for improvement in agricultural yield.

There are many such experimental methods of farming which could significantly increase output. Treatment plants that can turn garbage into food for shellfish farms have been developed. There are centers that feed worms raised on garbage to high-protein fish, such as trout, being produced in inland artificial lakes. Hydroponic farms that raise food in plastic greenhouses and reuse water and nutrients are now, according to futurist Herman Kahn, capable of "increasing the yield per acre by between 10 and 100 times." The technology is there. As Kahn asserts, feeding a world population five times that which we have now "is economically and technically feasible."

The same kinds of solutions are available, if we are resourceful enough, to eliminate future energy problems. Buckminster Fuller believes that it is possible to supply the entire world with abundant energy "while completely phasing out all further use or development of fossil fuels and atomic fusion energies." Fuller and Medard Gavel of the World Game Workshop in Philadelphia inventoried the entire world's known energy reserves, resources, and available technology and found that, if these three factors were combined and used properly, there was every reason to believe there is enough energy and resources to go around, even with the current rate of population increase.

Engineers are constantly able to do more with less. Fuller points out, for example, that in early telephone transmission, only one conversation could be sent per copper strand of telephone wire. With later developments, such as multiplexing, it became possible to send several hundred conversations per wire, thereby using less wire and less copper. With the advent of satellite communications and Comsat, it became possible to beam several thousand conversations to the satellite, thereby saving many more thousands of tons of copper. Now fiber optics technology is still further reducing our reliance of this limited resource. Essentially, the same story of technological advance is being retold in almost all of our significant nonreservable resources.

With new technology, energy can be harvested from the sun. Environmentalist Barry Commoner of Washington University in St. Louis states that although "we've all heard that solar energy is pie in the sky" and technologically very difficult, "this is simply not true"; in fact, a practical solar energy electrical generating system was displayed as long ago as 1904. In addition to solar energy, new technologies have been developed to obtain energy from the wind and tides, from hydrogen in water, from underground geothermal sources, from algae that can turn water into hydrogen fuel, from garbage that can be converted into burnable gas or alcohol, from materials that can turn cellulose (indigestible plant material) into alcohol, and other sources.

There are also ways to make our present utilization of energy more efficient. As Commoner says, "Presently we are able to maintain no better than 10 percent efficiency in converting energy . . . into work." He points out that with electrical production, for example, about 75 percent of the energy in the coal we use "goes up the stack as heat or into the river as waste hot water.'' In an electric hot water heater, only about 1 percent of the energy goes directly into making the water hot; the other 99 percent of the electricity is simply wasted. Designing and producing more efficient cars, manufacturing techniques, and heating devices will extend our resources. Commoner believes we can build machines that are at least two or three times as efficient as the ones we presently use.

Herman Kahn seems to sum up the position of those who disagree with the currently fashionable dismal view of the future: "At the Hudson Institute, we argue that we haven't approached the [population] limit, and won't in the foreseeable future. We see no reason why the world should not be able to support a population of 30 billion people with per capita earnings of $20,000 and with all the energy, raw materials, and food they need."

Even if we are incapable of completely replacing today's loose-jointed social and economic systems to arrive at an efficient, integrated system of food and energy production and distribution, there is still no reason to despair. If we can regulate the end of life with new antiaging techniques, so we can also regulate the beginning of it. More widely used and effective birth control techniques can be practiced, stabilizing the human growth rate at a level the world society finds acceptable, and constantly changing that level with the shifting values of the world at that time. Why should it be otherwise?

HANDLING THE SOCIAL PROBLEMS OF LONGEVITY

If, as it seems, by the end of the century a quarter of the U.S. population will be over sixty-five, we will unquestionably have to confront the social implications of that statistic long before we get there. The demand for health and social services is going to rise sharply whether or not investigation into antiaging and life extension continues.

If anything, such research should help to alleviate the social costs of aging. It is not the intention of those working in the forefront of gerontology to simply prolong life—it is to prolong *vigorous,* socially productive life. Robert Butler, director of the new National Institute on Aging and author of *Why Survive? Being Old in America* (which won the 1976 Pulitzer Prize for nonfiction), points out that "Much of what we think of as aging today is actually disease and illness, and not a part of fundamental physical aging." Many of the diseases of the elderly, for instance, result from deterioration of the immune system, and this can be forestalled. Other conditions associated with aging may result from vascular or neural disorders or even poor nutrition, and perhaps also can be reversed. But aging itself, Butler says, is not a disease.

If we can eliminate disease and illness in the aged and restore their vigor, then, we can erase a lot of the social costs of being old. The pressure on Social Security and pension funds, for instance, might be alleviated by raising the retirement age in many cases. Social Security defined sixty-five as a retirement age at a time, in the 1930s, when the number of people over sixty-five was about a third of the number today, and when average life expectancy was only about fifty-nine. While it is true that this might have some impact on the job market in terms of younger people trying to get into it, it must be noted still that today only about 16 percent of the people over sixty-five continue to work, as opposed to 38 percent in 1900.

According to the Administration on Aging, older persons at present are twice as likely to get sick and require hospitalization as are younger people. In addition, about 85 percent of older people have at least one chronic condition requiring some medical care. By keeping people healthier for longer periods, antiaging remedies could greatly reduce the need for medical services and perhaps also slow the rise in the costs of medical care.

It has been observed that we can barely pay for our health needs now, that the economics and planning side of medicine is bordering on chaos, and that to spend money on antiaging research represents a misguided sense of priorities. There is no question but what the service of our medical needs demands correction; however, antiaging research may not be an aggravation but in fact a benefit. The spinoff from it may alone justify its efforts. For example, the discovery of how cells age could well be applied to cancer research, for, unlike normal cells, cancer cells do not seem to be programmed for extinction after a certain number of proliferations. Discoveries originally aimed at solving one problem traditionally find application in other areas as well. The critics of the space program who thought that we were wasting hundreds of millions of dollars to get to the moon today enjoy the benefits of hundreds of earthbound products that have emerged from that research. As for the problem of life-extension benefits being available only to the very rich, we must remember that quite often in the history of science and invention the first benefits have been to the wealthy, but later, as demand increased, the innovation became available to all.

The worry that a nation of older voters would lead the country toward the right—might, indeed, elect as President a "man on horseback" who would return the country to the good old days—may be groundless, but in our youth-oriented society we tend to forget there is such a thing as "the wisdom of old age." For example, Butler points out that, though it was hardly given notice, Gallup polls from 1964 on showed that a greater proportion of people over fifty-five than of any other age group opposed American intervention in the Vietnam war. We by no means have all the answers—or even all the questions—as to the possible effects on society of the presence of a large class of vigorous, long-lived people. One wonders, however, if their power and influence could be any more misguided than that of any other dominant group that has governed and led societies in the past.

FREEDOM FROM DEATH

The most speculative area of all is what vigorous longevity will do to the individual human psyche, for it gives us an extraordinary gift: the gift of time. Many utopians believe that attainment of that time and leisure would allow mankind to develop its finest abilities, to explore literature and the arts, to advance the human species, to become like gods. With this extraordinary new freedom at hand we stand on the threshold of undreamed-of expansion of human possibilities, holding the gift not of life but of *lives.*

With a long life of youthful vigor, one could follow many careers, be a student of many disciplines, learn the skills of many arts, know and love many people. One could undergo many years of training to become a super-specialist, able to solve—and with the time to solve—seemingly intractible problems, such as those of disease, violence, and despoliation of the environment. One could survive centuries-long space flight and explore the limits of the universe.

But even the casual observers of humanity recognize that these are not the only choices that we can make, that for every height that man has reached there is a depth to which he has fallen.

As Caltech's Sinsheimer says, inquiry itself should not be exempt from inquiry. The application of the power of the atom has led mankind to within a hair's breadth of his own destruction. The field of recombinant DNA research is even more hazardous, for unlike fallout it is potentially self-perpetuating; synthetic living organisms are, by definition, self-reproducing. "We may be lucky," Sinsheimer says. "Nature may again protect us from our ignorance. I personally dislike to leave such a grave consequence in hostage to fortune."

But no matter how restrained we are in our scientific investigation, the fact is that it is not just a national matter, and it is likely that research would continue in countries other than our own. The 1975 Asilomar Conference was an important step toward agreeing on a consensus of policy as to how to handle a potentially very risky avenue of scientific inquiry. There must be many more such conferences. There could come a day when they will far surpass in importance this decade's Strategic Arms Limitations Talks. "The very success of science has ended its pleasant isolation," Sinsheimer states. "The impact of science and the increasing coupling of science to human affairs do encumber us with new responsibilities ... Somehow we need to be doubly responsible, both to mankind and to science, as one of man's finest creations. That will not be easy."

"The last enemy that shall be destroyed is death," it says in I Corinthians 15:26. And clearly the final assault is now under way.

Selected Bibliography

Asimov, I., *The Human Body*. New York: Signet, 1963.

Benet, S., *How To Live To Be 100: The Life-Style of the People of the Caucasus*. New York: Delacorte, 1976.

Billingham, R., and W. Silvers, *Immunobiology of Transplantation*. Englewood Cliffs, N.J.: Prentice-Hall, 1971.

Butler, R., *Why Survive? Being Old in America*. New York: Harper & Row, 1975.

Calne, R., *A Gift of Life*. New York: Basic Books, 1970.

Chambers, R. W., and J. T. Durkin, eds., *Alexis Carrel Centennial Conference*. Washington, D.C.: Georgetown University Press, 1973.

De Bouvoire, S., *The Coming of Age*. New York: Warner, 1973.

"Delphi Survey," Rand Corporation, Santa Monica, Calif., 1964.

Edwards, P. D., and W. S. Edwards, *Alexis Carrel, Visionary Surgeon*. Springfield, Ill.: Thomas, 1974.

Ettinger, R. C., *Man into Superman*. New York: Avon, 1974.

Fuller, R. B., *Earth Inc*. New York: Anchor, 1973.

———, *Synergetics*. New York: Anchor, 1975.

Galton, L., *How Long Will I Live?* New York: Macmillan, 1976.

Halacy, D. S., *Bionics*. New York: Holiday House, 1965.

———, *Genetic Revolution*. New York: Harper & Row, 1974.

Hardy, J., *Human Organ Support and Replacement*. Springfield, Ill.: Thomas, 1971.

Harrington, A., *The Immortalist*. New York: Avon, 1970.

Jacob, F., *The Logic of Life*. New York: Random House, 1973.

Kahn, H., *In the Year 2000*. New York: Morrow, 1976.

Karow, A., G. Abouna, and A. Humphries, *Organ Preservation for Transplantation*. Boston: Little, Brown, 1974.

Kugler, H., *Slowing Down the Aging Process*. New York: Pyramid, 1973.

Lozina-Lozinskii, L. K., *Studies in Cryobiology*. New York: Wiley, 1974.

McGrady, P., *The Youth Doctors*. New York: Macmillan, 1973.

Mertens, T. R., *Human Genetics: Readings on the Implications of Genetic Engineering*. New York: Wiley, 1975.

Miller, G. W., *Moral and Ethical Implications of Human Organ Transplants*. Springfield, Ill.: Thomas, 1971.

Moore, F. D., *Transplant*. New York: Simon & Schuster, 1972.

Moss, G., and W. Moss, eds., *Growing Old*. New York: Pocket Books, 1975.

Mrosovsky, N., *Hibernation and the Hypothalamus*. New York: Appleton-Century-Crofts, 1971.

Nolen, W., *Spare Parts for the Human Body*. New York: Random House, 1971.

Pauling, L., *Vitamin C and the Common Cold.* San Francisco: Freeman, 1970.
Prehoda, R. W., *Extended Youth.* New York: Putnam's, 1968.
——, *Suspended Animation.* Radnor, Pa.: Chilton, 1969.
Rockstein, M., ed., *Theoretical Aspects of Aging.* New York: Academic Press, 1974.
Rosenfeld, A., *The Second Genesis: The Coming Control of Life.* New York: Pyramid, 1972.
Selye, H., *The Stress of Life.* New York: McGraw-Hill, 1956.
Shifferes, J., *How to Live Longer.* New York: Collier, 1965.
Smith, A., ed., *Current Trends in Cryobiology.* New York: Plenum, 1970.
"Third Survey of Technological Breakthroughs and Widespread Application of Significant Technical Developments," Economics Department, McGraw-Hill Publications Company, New York, October 1972.
Young, J., *Cybernetics.* New York: American Elsevier, 1969.

Glossary

Antifreeze: Any chemical, such as glycerol, which, when present, lowers the freezing temperature of a cell solution or of the body and protects against ice-crystal formation.
B cells: Cells of the immune system. They produce antibodies, protein molecules which attack and kill living things such as bacteria which invade the body, and also neutralize certain toxic chemicals released by the invaders.
Catecholamine: Molecules released by the cells of the hypothalamus which are thought to regulate the pituitary gland. The pituitary in turn regulates other endocrine glands.
Cells: The units that compose all living things.
Cell membrane: The barrier surrounding cells, composed of proteins and fats. It regulates the movement of atoms and molecules into and out of cells.
Crosslinkages: Bridges that form in molecules of DNA, especially, which usually destroy the ability of the DNA to function.
Cytoplasm: The watery solution of proteins, fats, other organic molecules, and minerals contained inside the cell membrane of each cell.
DNA: Deoxyribonucleic acid, a long, twisted double chain of atoms found in the nucleus of each cell. It controls all the characteristics of living things, including metabolism in cells and body structure.
Endocrine glands: Organs in the body which control various body functions through the release of regulatory molecules called hor-

mones. Hormones exercise their control by influencing cellular metabolism. Examples are the pituitary and adrenal glands.

Enzymes: Those proteins found inside cells which drive most of the chemical reactions of metabolism.

Free radical: Any chemical that can, because of its highly chemically reactive nature, damage DNA, RNA, or protein.

Gene: A unit of DNA which contains the information necessary to produce one protein or one set of related proteins.

Genetic engineering: Any of a number of biological methods by which defective, damaged, or nonfunctional DNA can be altered or replaced. Also refers in a broad sense to any artificial manipulation of DNA, RNA, or protein.

Immune system: A group of organs and cells which protects the body from invasion by foreign living things (bacteria, fungi, viruses), and from altered body cells (cancer cells, or worn-out or damaged cells).

Immunosuppression: A medical method of preventing the immune system from attacking a transplant. Can be by means of X-rays, drugs such as Imuran and steroids, or through biological manipulation (with ALS).

Life expectancy: Average life expectancy is the age in years that any average individual may live (75 for human females, 68 for males). Maximum life expectancy is the greatest age, in years, that any person (or animal) has ever reached (believed to be 113 for humans).

Metabolism: The sum total of all chemical reactions occurring inside each cell, including those that provide the energy cells need, and those reactions that make proteins.

Nucleus: Lies in the center of each cell. Contains DNA, site of manufacture of RNA.

Organic molecules: Molecules that contain carbon atoms, in addition to other kinds of atoms. They are found in all living things, or as by-products of living things (such as oil). The main types are proteins, RNA, DNA, fats, and sugars.

Proteins: Long, folded chains of atoms found in the cytoplasm and cell membrane of cells. They are produced by RNA and serve two main functions: as enzymes and as structural components of cells and the bodies of living things.

Restriction enzymes: Enzymes obtained from bacteria. These enzymes can chop up any kind of DNA for use in genetic engineering experiments.

RNA; A long, twisted single chain of atoms found inside cells in the cytoplasm. It is produced by DNA and directs the formation of proteins.

T cells: Cells of the immune system. They primarily attack and kill cancer cells. They also assist B cells to produce antibodies.

Index